15-Minute Parenting

Joanna Fortune (MICP; MIFPP; Reg Pract APPI; CTTTS; ApSup PTI) is an accredited clinical psychotherapist and attachment specialist. She founded the Solamh Parent Child Relationship Clinic in Dublin in 2010 (www.solamh. com) where she works with families around a variety of issues. She is a recognised supervisor, trainer and conference speaker in her field. In 2017 she delivered a TEDx Talk on the topic 'Social media – the ultimate shame game?' Having previously written a parenting column for *The Sunday Times* she continues to write and contribute to articles on child development and parenting in various other print publications. She is also a regular media contributor to a variety of radio (RTÉ, Newstalk and regional radio) and TV shows (RTÉ and TV3). She is the parenting consultant on the weekly parenting slot on Newstalk's *Moncrieff*.

15-Minute Parenting

The Quick and Easy Way to Connect with your Child

Joanna Fortune

Gill Books

Gill Books
Hume Avenue
Park West
Dublin 12
www.gillbooks.ie

Gill Books is an imprint of M.H. Gill and Co.

© Joanna Fortune 2018

978 07171 8091 2

Design and print origination by O'K Graphic Design, Dublin
Edited by Jane Rogers
Proofread by Esther Ní Dhonnacha

Printed by ScandBook, AB Sweden
This book is typeset in 11/16 pt Adobe Caslon Pro with chapter
heading in Neutra Display.

*The paper used in this book comes from the wood pulp of managed forests.
For every tree felled, at least one tree is planted, thereby renewing natural
resources.*

A CIP catalogue record for this book is available from the British
Library.

5 4 3 2 1

Acknowledgements

When I was a child, my mother gave me a decorative bookmark that read: *you are a lover of words, one day you will write a book.* I held that nugget in my head as I grew up and am so grateful and excited that I have gotten to turn this belief into a truth.

I could list endless people who have inspired, believed in and encouraged me throughout my life and even saying that makes me feel very privileged indeed. Rather than write a list of people, I would like to acknowledge the important role that some people played in bringing this book to fruition.

My family who have never wavered in their support of every goal I have ever set myself. Thank you Mam, Dad, Joe, Robert, Kerrie, Aine, Anne and Emma.

My husband, who didn't even flinch when I said that I would write a book while on maternity leave and simply said, 'Of course you will,' and supplied endless encouragement and positivity … and child-free writing space.

My friends, my tribe of powerful women, whom I am so thankful for. A special mention for Joyce Fegan who listened to my book idea and suggested that I submit a proposal to Gill Books, regularly checked in and cheered on my word count progress and strongly advocated that this was indeed the perfect time to write a book.

Marianne Gunn-O'Connor for her helpful advice and feedback from the very early stages of this process.

My editor, Deirdre Nolan, who really got behind this book from the very beginning and indeed the entire Gill Books publishing team.

All of the children and families I have had the great privilege to work with throughout my career. Thank you for entering the wonderful world of play with me. I learned hugely from the therapeutic journey with each and every one of you.

Finally, and most importantly, to all of you reading this. Thank you for choosing this book and I sincerely hope it provides some ideas, clarity, fun, creativity and reassurance.

To Diarmuid and Masie, you are my world

Contents

15-minute parenting – what's it all about?

Don't we just wish that's all it took! But we all know that parenting is a 24/7 role and once we become parents our brains are hardwired to be on constant alert – attending to our children's needs, worrying if they're OK, if we are doing enough for them – all while we try to keep homes, jobs and family life working harmoniously.

I am not for one moment trying to dismiss the full-time nature of parenting but I am offering you an insight into what you can achieve in just 15 minutes of playtime with your children each day. It is because I fully appreciate the demands of parenting in busy families and lifestyles that I am showing you that small changes can and do make big differences.

But it's just play; what difference is that going to make?

There are countless psychosocial benefits for children (and parents) to spending time together as a family. Regular family time helps to create and sustain strong emotional connections between parents and children while keeping those all-important lines of communication open among all family members. Studies have shown that children who grow up in families where time together is a regular practice perform better at school and tend to display less challenging behaviours.

But how can I fit this in?

It is very difficult to feel as though you can build in enough quality family time when you are parents who work outside of the home and otherwise seem to be taxiing children between extracurricular activities. So what follows here is a parenting system based on simple but effective ways to build *quality* playful time together into any schedule, even when you might not have *quantity* time.

As best you can, keep family time together simple and fun; this way, you are more likely to keep it consistent and that is what matters most. It should not feel like a chore or yet another thing you have to fit into your day/week. If it does, perhaps you can tweak how you are doing it to ensure that it suits your family's definition of fun together. As long as it works for you and your family, it works!

To achieve this each day takes planning. You need to find a window each day of 15 uninterrupted minutes. If you can manage more, great, but 15 minutes is enough. Perhaps consider a longer play session (30 minutes or more) when you can all be at home together on a Saturday or Sunday afternoon. Pick three play activities for a 15-minute play time and perhaps five to seven activities for a 30-minute timeframe. Have anything you might need to hand so that you do not have to leave the room to get anything (most of the props I suggest are easily sourced around your home and do not require spending money). Turn off all phones and put a DO NOT DISTURB sign on the door. Be present.

The goal is fun, so all members of the family should be able to enjoy the activities you have planned. It's okay to play the same ones each week, but you can also mix it up a little and combine new games with familiar ones. It would be lovely if you could all play together like this every day but start with 15 minutes a few times a week, every week, and gradually build up. Being good enough is good enough!

....

Children don't want stuff from you – they want your time. Your presence is the best present you can offer. Take just 15 minutes a day with your child and you will build a connection, foster open communication and create memories that last a lifetime – it's child's play!

....

CHAPTER 1

Preparing for Parenting

History doesn't repeat itself, but it often rhymes. *How* we experienced being parented in our own childhoods will directly influence and inform the kind of parents we become to our own children. Our own early childhood experiences can leave us with a psychological scotoma, or mental blind spot, making us oblivious to what our own children need from us, particularly in the emotional areas of their lives.

We cannot nurture others if we feel un-nurtured ourselves. Insecurity in our own early attachments may contribute to a current sense of unfulfilment or disappointment. It is important that you value yourself enough to know that you must respond to this and take care of yourself so that you can take care of your child and respond to their needs in an attuned, securely attached way.

I believe that there is no better way of realising that you have unresolved issues from your own childhood than to become a parent. Becoming a parent and facing the daily demands and needs of a young child will bring unresolved issues bubbling to the surface and if we do not address these they will most certainly impact upon and influence the kind of parent we are to our own children. So parenting starts with introspection – looking inwards so that we can focus outwards beyond ourselves.

In these pages, I will be discussing the importance of raising our children to get them to a place where they can self-regulate their emotions, accepting that it is quite typical for this to take the first seven years of their lives; for children with added emotional and developmental needs it will take even longer. Self-regulation and the capacity to self-soothe are cornerstones of developing a capacity for intimacy and emotional closeness in relationships as we grow. However, this capacity is not an innate one. It is acquired, developed and nurtured within us through relationships we have with loving and caring others, primarily our own parents and then our extended attachment network (grandparents, relatives, childcare provider, a teacher, etc.). And so we must assume the role of imparting these essential life skills to our own children.

But how do we give what we didn't get ourselves? If you find it hard to welcome and embrace your child's emotional struggles, or if it's an effort to encourage and allow your child to separate from you so that they can explore their world while you observe from a distance and support their learning, there is a reason for this. Let's take a look at why.

PARENTAL SELF-AUDIT

Start by asking yourself some questions. The important thing is to answer as fully and honestly as you can, noting if there is something you feel requires further reflection or support to deepen your understanding. For some of us, this further reflection will be a personal contemplative process; for others, we may benefit from meeting with a suitably qualified professional who can support us in working through these blocks. It is important that your reflective process leads to practical actions you can take to address any blocks you might be experiencing. The play techniques detailed throughout this book will help you with this part of your process.

These questions might include:

- What was growing up like for you?
- In what ways was your relationship with your mother similar to/different from your relationship with your father?
- How were you disciplined as a child and how did this make you feel at the time? How do you feel about it now?
- Who played with you as a child? Do you have memories of your parents playing with and/or singing to you? Can you recall a specific time this happened? What was the game/song? How did it feel when they played with/sang to you? Or if they didn't, how does that feel to you now, and how might it have felt to you when you were young?
- Did you lose someone important to you through death or moving away? Who was this person and what was their role in your life?
- How were your successes celebrated in your family

when you were a child?

- How were your disappointments managed in your family when you were a child?

- Did you have important adults in your life outside your immediate family? Who were they? In what ways were they important to you?

- Did you ever feel unloved or unwanted by your parents? What impact did/does this have on you?

- Do you remember the first time you had to separate from your parents (for at least one day and one night)? How did this feel for you at the time? What was it like when you returned to your parents?

- What would happen when you were sick (so sick you had to stay off school, for example)?

- What would happen when you were hurt (such as falling and cutting your knee)?

- When you think of someone who provided you with comfort and nurture, who comes to mind?

- Did you feel loved as a child? By whom?

- What is your saddest memory from your own early childhood?

- What is your happiest memory from your own childhood?

- When did you realise that you loved your own child? Do you still love them?

- Name three things that you want your child to grow up believing above anything else.

Now write a list of five things that bring you pleasure. These should be things that are about *you*, not about your child or how they might bring you pleasure. Your list might include things like:

- swimming
- running
- football
- golf
- painting/art and crafts
- dinner with friends
- a hot stone massage/blow-dry/facial/nail treatment/haircut/hot towel shave, etc.
- a night away alone with your partner.

Now ask yourself when was the last time you got to do each of the things that bring you pleasure. Can you build time into your week to ensure that you do at least one of these things each week? If you can't, ask yourself what needs to change/shift in order for you to be able to.

Next, consider how you are currently parenting your child(ren) (if you have more than one child you will have to repeat this for each child – every child is different and how you parent each of them will also be at least slightly different). Ask yourself the following questions:

- Do I find opportunities each day to tell my child that I love them and that I am proud of them?
- Do I give my child opportunities to practise independence? Am I developing these opportunities in line with their development?

- Am I able to be firm yet gentle with my child when necessary?
- Am I safe, predictable, calm and consistent in how I interact with and respond to my child?
- Do I follow my child's lead where possible, but take charge when necessary?
- Do I have the opportunity to laugh at least once a day with my child? Does my child feel that I enjoy them?
- Do I seek to know the best bit of my child's day and what bit of their day they would like to change?
- Do I encourage my child to try new things and to take (appropriate) risks?
- Do I praise their efforts over any outcomes?
- Do I show empathy when my child seeks my help/support/protection and comes to me for hugs/kisses?
- Did I experience repair/recovery following a rupture with my child today (perhaps not every day)?
- Do I play with my child for 15 minutes each day?
- Do I ensure we have a bedtime story together each night no matter what else has/hasn't happened?

A parental self-audit is not a one-time reflection. This is an exercise that you can and should repeat as your child grows up.

CHAPTER 2

Child-proofing Your Relationship

Something rarely spoken about when we discuss the topic of parenting is how parenthood impacts on our intimate partner relationships. Becoming parents is stressful, even if it's not your first time or first child. Added to that is the fear that we are not *good enough*. But what happens after the birth of your first baby is particularly significant and can set the trajectory for your journey through parenthood and how you adjust within your intimate partner relationships to accommodate the role of parenthood.

Children (should you choose to have them) should be *an* important part of your family, but they should never be *the most* important part of your family. This may seem like a controversial statement, but I do not intend it to be so. What I mean is that children should grow up seeing that every member of their family is valued, appreciated and important. The overall family dynamic and your relationship with each other is the most important aspect of building a family. Becoming parents is the hardest thing a couple will go through together. It is vital that they find ways to go on the journey together, but this is not always easy. Expectations rarely align with reality and there is a very real adjustment period that can take anything up to three years. The transition to parenthood should not be at the cost of your relationship. Many couples I have spoken with talk about the challenging transition from being a couple to being pregnant and then having a child.

The process of becoming a parent is a very different one from the perspective of the non-pregnant parent. Pregnancy allows prospective mothers to bond and connect and begin to attach to their fantasy babies, preparing them to love the real baby. The first four months of co-dependency is really mother–baby time, psychologically speaking. This can result in the other parent feeling as if they are on the outside looking in. We have to change how we speak about this. The very important role for the other parent is to support the mother so that she can be as available to her baby as the baby needs her to be, and this is not an insignificant role.

Pregnancy is so all-consuming, physically and emotionally, that it is not uncommon for a couple to not really think about what it will be like when pregnancy ends and the baby comes home. Most couples find that they are faced with renegotiating their relationships after a baby arrives, which is difficult to do given everything else that is going on in the post-partum period (the first eight weeks). The hope is that this can be done in an open and communicative way, resulting in vast improvements … after some initial adjustments, of course. The amount of time needed for these adjustments varies for different couples, from a few months to close to a year, or longer. Most couples spend a lot of energy trying to adapt to life with a new baby who has 'changed everything'. Finding time for your non-parent selves, as individuals and as a couple, and trying to pursue lifestyle activities you enjoyed before becoming parents is not easy but it is important.

Birth preparation classes stop with the delivery of your baby. Unless you proactively undertake to source and take a parenting course, which you are unlikely to do when you are in the throes of your post-partum experience and are just trying to manage a new-born and the associated sleep deprivation, you will not have that extra support. Anxiety is so common in these early parenting days and none of us are our best selves when we are full of anxious anticipation. This also impacts on our relationship with each other.

My wish for everyone who decides to become a parent is that they are encouraged to invest in child-proofing their relationship and preparing for parenthood rather than spending thousands of euro on a top-end buggy or designer nursery furniture. There are stages in the process of blending parenthood into your relationship – or child-proofing your relationship – but we must start by accepting that we cannot possibly know what we do not know.

Pre-conception, when we are trying for a baby, and during pregnancy, when we are expecting a baby, what is happening to our changing bodies is all-consuming. Then we attend antenatal classes and the focus is on delivering the baby. But right up to the moment when your new baby is placed in your arms (when the focus shifts to how you will feed the baby), nobody talks to you about how your relationship with each other will feel once the baby comes home with you and two become three. It's almost as though we are expected to get home and just automatically adjust without any adverse or lasting impact upon our relationship with each other or the baby.

Our culture sets people up for failure when it comes to parenting and maintaining relationships. We are juggling multiple roles and the shiny veneer of social media can give us the (very false) impression that we must manage it all while smiling in our leisure wear, pushing a designer buggy, sipping a latte and taking gorgeous family selfies declaring how happy we all are. It's okay to not be okay ... but that doesn't look as good on social media.

THE POST-PARTUM PERIOD

Emotionally we take a bit of a battering in the first year of parenting. Between hormones, sleep deprivation, and attuning and responding to the constant and evolving needs of a new-born baby, we can end up feeling lost without a roadmap to tell us whether we are going in the right direction. This makes us extremely emotionally vulnerable. If we know ahead of time that this will happen (not 'might' – it really will happen), we can better identify, empathise with and support each other's emotional vulnerability. This will also help us to normalise it as a stage of the process of adjusting to parenthood, and it won't feel so overwhelming in the moment.

We can become so focused on responding to every need our new baby might have that we can often do so at a cost to our own needs and those of our partner. Babies (typically but certainly not universally) settle into a routine of sorts between four and six months of age. This is a good time to set aside some time for yourself and each other. Enlist a couple of hours' babysitting from friends or family who have offered to help and take yourselves out to dinner. This time in parenthood is about really focusing on what matters, the simple, small things (healthy food, a walk alone, a bath, a trip to the hairdresser, meeting up with friends for an hour or two, as well as grabbing some time for and with each other as a couple) and ensuring that we communicate these needs to each other. When we name and address our own needs we are better able to recognise and respond to those needs in those we care about.

As new parents we can find ourselves staring at an unrecognisable version of ourselves in the mirror wondering who we are and how we got here. This is compounded when we feel as if we are failing at parenthood because it doesn't feel anything like the photos and online posts. We can suffer a loss of identity, a drop in self-esteem and terrible loneliness. Support from one's partner is crucial in turning this around, but it can take 18 months and more for this roller-coaster to settle and slow down. Feeling that your partner believes that you are a good enough parent is a big factor.

It is no surprise that conflict and tension between parents can make young babies and toddlers feel emotionally unsettled, in turn causing them to act out. Perhaps you didn't truly understand each other's position on parenting and raising children ahead of time. When those differences emerge they can cause tension, and you may enter a power struggle you hadn't anticipated. Ideally we would sit down with our partner during the pre-conception planning for a baby stage and discuss our thoughts and beliefs about raising happy and secure children, but this doesn't always happen. However, it is never too late to have that conversation, starting with how each of you was raised and how you experienced that and what lessons you are carrying forward into your own parenting. This is about the art of compromise, accepting that neither of you is fully right or fully wrong but knowing that together you can reach an agreed parenting plan.

A large percentage of parents report relationship dissatisfaction during the first three years of their child's life. Depending on how you deal with the other aspects of the adjustment to parenthood, having a baby will either bring you closer together or drive a wedge between you. This is not the baby's responsibility, but more about the process of becoming parents. And these adjustments will not just be relevant in the first three years of parenting, because as soon as you feel that you have it worked out, your children will only go and grow up a stage and you will find yourself having to readjust while trying to work out differences, empathise and support each other and find time for your relationship all over again. But remember that while it can feel as though the baby is the master of your home, you and your partner are the glue that holds the whole thing together. So learn to reach out, share your vulnerability with each other, say what you need, empathise and support one another and take up the babysitting offers so that you can get out, just the two of you, and reconnect with each other.

SELF-CARE

I have met with countless parents who exclaim that they no longer recognise themselves since they became parents, that they've lost sense of who they were before this life-changing event. It is not that they resent or regret their parental role, more that they're wondering who they are now and who they are to each other as a couple now that they are parents.

Nothing shocks me more than when a parent tells me that they haven't been away from their children overnight in three or four years – this is not a one-off story, either! Not only is this not in a parent's best interests; it is not in the child's best interests either.

The first four to six months of a baby's life is a time of co-dependence. They have not yet understood that they are a separate being to their mother. This is a time when your child does need as much of you as you can give in terms of physical presence. But at between 12 and 18 months, when your child begins the transition from object to people permanence, is when you must begin to give them distance, space and the opportunity to miss you.

It is important to get some skin-to-skin contact when you are reunited – a hand, a stroke of the face, a hug, a kiss, whatever works for you – as this is a sensory reconnection and is calming for your child, reassuring them that you are back. Their people permanency process should begin with you leaving a room for a brief period of time, and building up to leaving the home for couple of hours. Then they will be better prepared for a more prolonged absence such as a full day at crèche or you heading away for an overnight break.

Even after the 18-month stage, when they have a better grasp of the fact that you exist even when they cannot see you, it is good for children to see their parents have a life away from them. To see you go and come back is reassuring for them, particularly in the long run.

Taking care of ourselves, our relationships, our friendships, and investing in having an identity beyond being a parent is not only important to us as parents and people but is also a good way to model self-care for our children as they grow and develop. Taking time for yourself and nurturing your non-parent self will help you to be the type of parent you want to be because you will be better able to cope with the day-to-day stresses of parenthood. Far from feeling guilty about wanting time away from your children for yourself, it is something that you should do and it is in their interests, developmentally, too. It might also make you happier, and a happier parent means happier children!

Here are some tips for planning some time out for your non-parent self.

Have a **date night**, just the two of you, once a week or every fortnight. You can do this with a friend or family member too. Banning talk of the children at dinner isn't realistic, but you should certainly agree that you won't only speak of the children. Talk to each other about what is happening at work, talk about something that happened that made you laugh, shocked you or gave you a great idea ... Have fun and laugh together!

If you are lucky enough to have someone (friend or family) who will take your children for a **weekend** or an overnight once in a while, take them up on the offer and arrange it in advance – the better planned you are, the easier it will be for you to switch off while you're away. Spend this time together investing in each other and your relationship, or if you're doing it alone, grab a friend and invest in yourself and your friendships.

Join a **book club** or something similar, giving you a set evening each month when you get together with friends and discuss something other than your children. Get out for a walk together, or alone ... trust me, it's a different experience when you're not pushing a buggy or watching a couple of children.

REDISCOVERING PLAY

When it comes to bringing more playfulness into your own adult life and relationships you need look no further than your own children for inspiration. Children can literally make a game out of anything (a nine-month-old with a cardboard box will show you that) and they find delight and pleasure in all things magical and creative. Children are also very wise; they are great at identifying who in their world is playful, and they will quickly seek out these people to engage with. They can transition seamlessly from seriousness to playfulness and in this regard we have a lot to (re-)learn from our children. I say re-learn as we have all been children once and I believe the capacity to be playful exists within all of us; we just may have to dig deep to find it if we have gone rusty. If you read this and think, 'Gosh, it's been twenty or thirty years since I've really played,' it is entirely possible to start playing now and to use it as a means to have more fun in your relationship with your partner and your children, resulting in fewer tears and more laughter for everyone in the family. Let's make a commitment to find ways to prioritise playfulness and make play an essential part of your family life.

But first, let's look at some practical ways to bring play and playfulness back into your adult relationships. A good place to start is to spend time just watching your children play. Because play is not just an activity but a state of mind, you will immediately see their unabashed, uninhibited enthusiasm, so take inspiration from that and approach playfulness in your own relationship with the same positive and open outlook.

If you feel that this does not describe where you currently are in your relationship, but perhaps you once were and would like to try to get back to that place or even somewhere like it, be assured that you can learn this way of being and it starts with giving some of the games a go. We can make a conscious choice to be more attentive, responsive and attuned partners and become more mindful of each other's needs and desires. Breaking old habits is not simple or straightforward, but it is possible to consciously rewire our ingrained neural pathways and develop new ways of being and relating with each other. Sometimes this requires the help of a suitably qualified and accredited professional, but it can start with getting back to basics and getting back to play. If we can play with each other, we can play with our children and teach them that playfulness is truly a state of mind.

15-minute practice: Rediscovering play

Stay with me on this one. I appreciate it takes a leap of faith to do some of it without feeling entirely silly, but then again, the benefits of being entirely silly are a bedrock of this book and you don't have to use all these ideas – even one is a start.

Turn chores into games. So you have to wash the dishes, not all that exciting, right? But if one of you washes while the other dries you can roleplay being movie characters or interviewer/interviewee or sports commentators ... think along the lines of 'Tom takes the bowl, still dripping wet, and passes it to Ann, who wraps it in a tea towel before stacking it on the sideboard,' or 'So tell me, Tom, how did you prepare for this role of Cinderella? Had you done much housework previously?' You're doing the dishes anyway, why not have a laugh in the process?

Challenge each other to come up with **one joke each day** and see who can make the other laugh hardest.

Try a version of **hide and seek** to bring some more affection and nurture into it. Leave your partner a surprise note telling them one thing you love about them or a memory you thought of from your dating days that made you smile, and/or a chocolate or sweet by their pillow for them to find.

If you are driving or travelling on a train or bus together, play a game of **'I went on a picnic and I brought ...'** (If you're not familiar with this, each person adds one item to the list of things brought and when it is your turn you must recite the entire list before adding a new item to the end of it.)

Choose a favourite passage from a book you love, or your favourite children's book from your own childhood, or some poetry, and **read to each other**, perhaps sharing what you love so much about this particular piece or narrative.

We might talk all the time, especially when we have children and we are using cognitive connection and verbal instructions and planning, but we rarely touch. And I mean **touch without an agenda**. Touch has healing and soothing powers; it lowers blood pressure and reduces anxiety, so it is very helpful in busy households and relationships where you can feel like ships passing in the night. Try a hug, playfully grabbing each other, tickling, playful (and gentle) wrestling or even just holding hands while sitting or lying side by side. A study conducted by James Coan, a neuroscientist at the University of Virginia, found that the reassuring touch of someone you truly love and feel loved by can affect your physiological experience of pain[1]. His study found that if you're in a healthy relationship, holding your partner's hand is enough to reduce your blood pressure, ease your response to stress, improve your health and soften physical pain. A touch from a loved one can and does alter one's physiological and neural functions.

RELATIONSHIP BREAKDOWN

When an adult relationship breaks down it is often difficult and stressful for the adults involved, who need time and space to grieve the loss of the relationship and process what the end of the relationship means to them. This is further complicated when you have children together because even though you have decided you do not wish to be together any more, you are faced with having to stay involved in each other's lives because you are involved with the children you both love.

Agreeing a successful co-parenting strategy when your feelings towards each other might be fraught is very difficult, and it can be a good idea to find a qualified mediator to support you. Very young children (under seven years old) really need their relationships with both of their parents to be predictable, consistent and reliable. Being exposed to parental conflict at this young age can frighten and overwhelm them because they cannot make sense of it, so they (and their relationship with both parents) need to be protected from this conflict in order to safeguard their secure attachment to both parents. Very young children struggle to manage long separations from their primary attachment figures, so regular (and consistent, predictable and reliable) access to both parents is essential to their healthy social and emotional development. Having a contact schedule can be reassuring for all involved as it provides that all-important structure and predictability. Of course it is equally important to build in room for flexibility because life happens and there will be times when one of you needs the schedule to change to accommodate unforeseen events.

In addition to a contact schedule, you may be faced with the fact that your partner's parenting style is different from yours. Children do best when their parents are consistent in their responses to them and are at least mostly on the same page. This won't always be possible and even if things are mostly consistent there will be some differences.

Try to avoid picking faults with each other's parenting and ask yourself before you say anything, 'Am I irritated because this is not how I choose to parent or because it does not meet an essential need for our child?' For example, you might prefer that your child is not playing outside after 5 p.m. when the evenings get damp and cold. This is a parenting preference. On the other hand, your child having to take their asthma inhalers at set times of the day with both parents is an essential need. Essential needs must happen and as long as your child is safe and well you will have to tolerate your parental preferences not always being followed when your child is in the care of their other parent.

Children are very attuned to their parents' emotions and responses, so they will be watching you to see how you feel about the other parent. If they think talking about mummy/daddy upsets you they will stop talking about them. If you can tolerate it, it can be nice for your child to have framed photos of themselves with the other parent in both homes. If you can manage a positive and upbeat (even brief) discussion about what they did with the other parent during the week/weekend, this will also help, and young children will need your support, help and encouragement to send the other parent messages/make phone calls during the week/weekend. It is also important that both parents know about significant events in their child's life. These could include a spelling test they are anxious/proud about, passing their speech and drama exam, learning the backstroke in swimming or having fallen out with a friend. Ensure that both of you have a copy of dates and times of events in your child's life that require both of you to be there. These will range from parent–teacher meetings to big match days.

All of this requires calm and consistent communication between parents. When your child is with their other parent you will find yourself with time to yourself. On the one hand, this might sound fabulous; but on the other, some parents can find it sad or lonely. Reconnect with your friends, or your old hobbies/passions/interests, and make a plan to see a movie. Take care of yourself and attend to what you need to get you through any difficult patches as you adjust to this new way of life for your family.

A lot of what I am writing here is from the perspective of what is best for your young child after parental separation, and I am aware that I am presenting an ideal situation when life is not always ideal. If your child does see or hear you having a blazing row, engage in repair as soon as you can afterwards. 'Mummy and daddy had a row because we are not getting on very well at the moment. I'm sorry you had to see/hear that; we were both feeling cross and we shouldn't have said those things to each other. We both love you very much and will work harder on making things nicer for all of us to get along' – or words to that effect. Focus, as always, on getting it mostly right most of the time and *good enough being good enough.*

If you are co-parenting within a blended family structure there are a few more considerations to bear in mind. In a blended family, two or more families come together in new relationships to make a new, bigger family unit. It may have looked like the Brady Bunch in your head, but the reality is often quite different, at least initially. Be aware that developing a healthy blended family structure starts off with challenges. You can anticipate that numerous members of the family unit(s) will struggle, and it is important to be sensitive to that and to try to consider it from the perspective of everyone affected.

Like with co-parenting, ensure that you make a clear plan of what is expected from everyone involved in relation to childcare, participation in family events or events in the children's lives, and factor in time for you and your new partner away from the children. Give your ex-partner notice that you are introducing somebody new into your and your children's (and ultimately their) lives. Do not discuss this emotionally, but say that you would like to discuss it when they have had time to think it through; and book some time to do so. Try to agree on a shared parenting strategy whereby you are all (at least mostly) on the same page, while bearing in mind that you and your ex-partner are still the parents of your children and you must work to be united on this front, even if it means pushing your personal differences aside. Anticipate bumps on the road and plan for these by allowing for a respectful adjustment period for all involved. This is much easier said than done, so consider working it all through with a trained mediator, if you feel that would help.

If you don't love each other anymore, work on liking each other so that your children see your mutual respect and mirror the same towards both of you. This might be difficult in some families, so start small and find one or two things about how your ex-partner parents your children that you like and respect; focus on that, and find more things like that. Focusing on one positive thing will be more helpful in building a mutually respectful co-parenting front than listing the myriad things the other person does that drive you mad. Try to agree on three to five positive family values you can both uphold, with and for your children, even when you are living separately. For example, 'In our family we take time to care about each other's feelings; we have fun together; we talk to each other about what is happening in our lives; we play together; we show respect for everyone.' Once you have an agreed list it can be a good idea to write it up, print and laminate it and stick it somewhere visible to everyone so that the same list of family values is upheld in both homes by both parents.

You may have decided to split, but do not allow your children to split between you. Never keep a secret about the children from the other parent and ensure that they know that you wouldn't. They want and need to know that they still have you both in your lives and that even if you do not love each other in the way you once did, you will always have in common your shared love of them.

If you are parenting alone, all of the above (and what is coming next) still stands, but you face the added challenge of not having a co-parent to help you negotiate the day-to-day stuff. Reach out to your own family network, if they are available to you, and when people offer to help out, get good at saying 'Yes, please' and assigning them a task: 'It would really help if you could take him to his football match this weekend,' or 'It would be great if you could babysit for an evening', etc. You have a much busier parent-load to carry, so take help where you can and be sure to build and access your family/friend network to help get you through.

Whether you are parenting together, co-parenting apart, co-parenting within a blended family structure or parenting alone, what your children want and need from you remains the same. Children, whatever their age, want to know that they have access to safe, predictable, loving, calm and consistent parent(s)-in-charge who will make the world a safe and exciting place for them as they grow and develop.

CHAPTER 3

Getting Started and Being Good Enough

Before we get stuck into the practical play techniques that I want to share with you in this book, it is important to lay some solid foundations upon which we can build. This chapter is all about helping you to shine a light inwards and deepen your understanding of your own parenting impulses from the inside out. This will help you develop the tools you will need to build a framework for what follows.

Let's start from a place of affirmation. Good enough is good enough. And if you can embrace this as your starting point, there is room to make mistakes in parenting. More than that, you understand that making mistakes as a parent is important in modelling the value of repair and recovery for your children. Modelling perfection does not promote healthy development, so give yourself a break; it's okay not to have all the answers all the time. You will also accept that it is never too late to move towards a parenting model based on fewer tears and more laughter. Accepting this enables you to embrace new ways of parenting that will result in positive outcomes for both you and your child.

I believe that most parents are doing the very best that any of us can. I believe that we all possess what we need to parent our children to a good enough level. Some of us will benefit from support to access the capacity and potential that lies within us, because sometimes it lies beneath years of carefully scaffolded defensive layers, which are blocking us from being the best kind of parent we can be. Your parental self-audit is intended to help you look inwards and shine a light on some of this 'stuff', but bear in mind that some of the stuff lurking in the shadows requires support from a trained professional who can help us identify, process and integrate the learning from negative experiences so that we can move forward.

What is called *good enough* parenting is determined by our intentions. If our intentions are good and genuine they will help us to form safe, secure and lasting attachments with our children. This also creates a solid foundation of procedural memory in our children. Procedural memory is like a breadcrumb trail we leave in our children's psyche as they grow and develop, and it serves as a soothing and encouraging kind of internal soundtrack that influences the choices they make, the things they do, the friendships and relationships they form; in fact everything that happens as they grow out of childhood into adolescence and then into adulthood. Your ability to emotionally self-regulate allows you to co-regulate with your child and ultimately to lead them to be able to emotionally self-regulate by the time of middle childhood. It's a bit like riding a bike. Once you know how to do it you don't need to run through the steps in your mind before setting off – you simply get up on the bike and go. This is how procedural memory works. We learn how to think/feel/behave, we store that in our procedural memory bank and then we just get on with it.

True wisdom and security and a positive sense of self lie in how our feeling brain (limbic system) and our thinking brain (prefrontal cortex) connect and communicate with each other. The key to the way they connect and communicate is held in our procedural memory. That is what good enough parenting is about – filling up that procedural memory bank for and with your children. When you meet your child's needs and respond to their demands with appropriate, calm and consistent boundaries and limit-setting in the first two years of life, you are investing in their procedural memory bank and helping them to develop memories that will stand to them throughout their life, growing them into emotionally resilient and self-regulating adults.

Learning how to self-regulate our emotions is an essential life skill without which we cannot function as healthy adults. When you see your child engaging in so-called 'acting-out' behaviours (or, conversely, 'acting-in' behaviours, when they turn emotions inward against themselves), what you are actually witnessing is your child's attempts to manage their emotions when they don't have the requisite life skills to do so. Dysregulated emotions result in dysregulated behaviour, and if you only respond to the behaviour without considering the emotional disruption you are not addressing the real problem. Purely behavioural modification parenting techniques might change the overt behaviour, but in my clinical experience

I tend to see children re-presented for treatment with a new behavioural issue and the same underlying emotional dysregulation. We must get to the emotional kernel of the matter to effect meaningful and sustained change in behaviour.

MENTALISATION

So how do you manage this in the busyness of day-to-day parenting? The answer lies in increasing your mentalisation around your child. Mentalisation is a psychological term that describes the process of holding a mind in mind. What this means is that in thinking and reflecting about your child's behaviours and experiences and how they are impacting on you, you can also and at the same time consider, wonder and reflect about the same things from your child's perspective. What might they have been thinking and feeling when this happened? Where might those thoughts and feelings stem from? Is there an emotional trigger, a sensory trigger or even a physical trigger? I am a fan of ruling out the physical first so I would suggest quickly assessing whether your child could be hungry or thirsty or tired. If the answer to any of these is 'yes', respond to that physical need first. When children are physically dysregulated it directly impacts on their emotional and, by association, behavioural states of being.

When you have determined possible physical triggers, you need to try to make connections as to how and why your child behaviourally acted out in a given situation. For example:

My child had a temper tantrum in the shopping centre (**child's overt behaviour**) <u>because</u> I had been walking them around the shops all day and they had had enough (**child's emotional state**) and they needed a nap (**child's physical state**).

Here you are considering your child's acting-out behaviour as it is connected to their physical and emotional states. We cannot treat these in isolation because they are connected. This is how our children function.

In their very early life children make no distinction between their work and their play because their play is their work; it is what matters most to them. When they play they are working very hard developing crucial life skills and negotiating developmental hurdles. They go at the things that matter to them and hold meaning for them with great gusto and single-minded devotion – whether that's collecting snails from the garden, building with Lego, drawing a picture, reading a book, making up a story, feeding the goldfish or watering a plant. It does not matter who has asked them to do a task, whether it is their parent, teacher, grandparent or childminder, because what matters more to them is that they find the assigned task interesting and engaging. Even if they find the task difficult and challenging they will engage in it fully because it's more important to them than a less interesting but more attainable task. So when they seem as though they are not listening to our instructions, do not assume it is an act of defiance; it may be that they are simply absorbed in a task that is super-interesting for them and their behaviour is their way of telling us that they are not ready to do whatever it is we're asking.

Of course, sometimes we really do need them to stop building Lego and find their other shoe so that everyone can get out of the door and to school on time. But if we understand what they're thinking it will change *how* we make our request. Perhaps turning the missing shoe into a mystery to be solved or a treasure hunt is the most creative and effective way to get our own needs met without having a row first thing in the morning. We may also be able to approach our children by naming their experience for them, to show them that we understand what is happening for them, thus deepening their own understanding of why they find our requests intrusive and frustrating when they are hard at work ... playing. Something like this might prove helpful: 'I know you're very busy building a town right now and you would much rather be doing that when I need you to join us at the table for dinner. Let's all sit together for dinner and have a chat and if you come straightaway you will still have time to play after dinner.'

RUPTURE AND REPAIR

Rupture and repair are key elements of all healthy relationships. It is important to make mistakes so that we can learn from them because a rupture followed by a repair allows for growth to take place, and children are about growing. A rupture happens when you get frustrated and yell at your child or send them away to another room rather than sitting with them and seeking to better understand their feelings. A rupture can happen when you wave your child away from you while you are on the phone when they are bursting to tell you something. A rupture can happen when you are away from your child all day and they miss you. In other words, ruptures happen in all parent–child relationships and are perfectly normal.

What matters most is that we follow this up by making a repair and that we do so quickly. This involves coming down to your child's eye level and taking responsibility where appropriate, for example:

- ⊕ 'I was angry and frustrated and I didn't pay attention to how you were feeling. I'm sorry I sent you away to another room. I wonder what that was like for you.'
- ⊕ 'You wanted to show/tell me something and I couldn't pay attention to you because I was on the phone and I waved you away. That must have felt harsh to you. I'm here now and I'd love to know what you want to tell me.'
- ⊕ 'It's so hard to be apart all day; you missed me and I missed you too. Even though we weren't together I was thinking about you in my head and I thought about that time when we [insert a nice memory] and that made me smile. Maybe you could try that when you feel sad that we are not together. Let's play a game together now.'

Developing an understanding that good things (repair) follow bad things (rupture) is important in your child's emotional development and helps them to grow into more resilient people. It also helps them to better manage disagreements they have with their own friends because they know how to make a repair. Knowing how to make a repair following a rupture in a relationship is a vital life skill for anyone to learn.

As adults we can fall into a pattern of insisting we are right, so saying 'sorry' and actually meaning it can be difficult. Perhaps we view saying sorry as undermining our parental authority and weakening us in the eyes of our child. But the converse is true: in making repair we are modelling strength of character and upholding the strength in our relationship. That said, if you are not feeling sorry you are not ready to say it. Better to wait a little and reflect on what you are feeling and why than to approach your child with 'Fine, I'm sorry I shouted, but you shouldn't have ...' because blame has no place in repair; indeed, blame actively blocks the road to repair. And when I say blame I mean both blaming your child for what happened and also blaming yourself and seeing what happened as evidence that you are a bad parent, which will send you spiralling into shame, from where authentic repair cannot be made. So don't rush in to make an inauthentic repair but take time to reflect on what is keeping you in a blame space.

Reflection is good, but you need to follow it up with resolution. It's no good simply reflecting on it all inwardly and patting yourself on the back for great self-reflection if you omit the resolution part and leave your child in a state of rupture for a prolonged period of time. It is perfectly okay to approach your child a little later and say something like 'I needed some time to think about what happened and how I was feeling about it. I understand now why I yelled and I'm sorry that I did that. I love you always, no matter what you do, and even if I'm cross with you. Can you help me understand what you were thinking and feeling when this happened?'

Now, don't overdo it either. Be aware if you are apologising all the time for every little thing that happens and treating every feeling your child has as the most important thing in the world. If you are constantly apologising, your apologies may become empty and be met with a shrug or an eye-roll because 'so what?' Every time you give out does not equal a rupture and sometimes you are making quick repairs as you go: 'Come on, stop it! [Move straight to their eye level with hands held] I think you forgot how we do that in this family; would you like to try it again? [Child does well] I'm proud of you for making a better choice.' This does not require further reflection and an apology because the repair was automatic.

If you parent in an over-sensitive way and over-respond to every feeling your child has you will struggle to stay in charge and your child will spot that weakness in you. Children who actually want their parents to take charge often communicate this by pushing limits, provoking you to act. Renowned attachment researcher John Bowlby talked about how children need their parents to be bigger, stronger and wiser and I take this to mean that children need us to be the safe, calm, consistent and predictable parent-in-charge who can show understanding and acceptance and make sense of their emotional world with and for them when the wheels come off and they fall apart now and then.

Remember, what can look like a demand for attention is often a need for connection and very often a child's negative behaviour is their confused, overwhelmed and mixed-up way of seeking that connection. This is why repair following rupture is so crucial to their social and emotional development. Now give yourself a break because good enough is always good enough, so if you get this rupture/repair process mostly right most of the time then you are doing good enough!

REFLECTIVE FUNCTIONING

Children need to feel heard and understood as they grow up. It helps them to learn. It helps them to co-regulate and eventually self-regulate their own emotions. It is good for their self-esteem that they feel important and that what they have to say matters to you. And ultimately it helps them to develop the important reflective functioning skills that we all need as we negotiate our way through life. Reflective functioning is a clinical term coined by the psychoanalyst Peter Fonagy and colleagues in their research[2]. It is the ability to understand not only ourselves but also one another. It requires that we seek to imagine what the other person might be thinking or feeling about a given situation.

This is an important life skill for lots of reasons, not least because it enables us to read a situation and the people in it and gauge our response accordingly. It also allows us to know ourselves while also being able to read how other people are experiencing us (what we are doing/saying) and to change our own behaviour to elicit a different response from them. It relies on understanding a set of internal mental states such as intentions, feelings, thoughts, desires and beliefs, both in others and in ourselves. It is also the ability to recall a situation from the past with fresh thinking and a new perspective. You will see evidence of this as your child grows when they can tell you about an event that happened previously (days, weeks, months, even years ago) and as they re-tell it you observe that they can think about it differently, perhaps showing that they were upset *then* but understand what happened and feel calmer about it *now*. They should not be as upset in the re-telling as they were at the time the event happened.

To use reflective functioning in your parenting strategies you must try to remain open and curious and avoid slipping into a place of 'knowing'. Rather, always 'seek to know' more about a person or situation. This is not easy because as parents we are often wired to believe that we should know everything, be the authoritarian in-charge parent (of course you can be the parent-in-charge, which is important, without being authoritarian) and we sometimes tell our child what they are thinking and feeling rather than supporting them in developing that insight themselves. It is very useful to regularly examine your own thoughts, feelings, desires, strengths and areas you identify as growth areas for yourself. Explore the same with your child by being open and curious and seeking to better understand these mental states in them while also taking the time to discuss a range of issues, any concerns you might have about how they are behaving, and identifying together some actions that they/you can take to make things work better for everyone.

You will find that you use 'wondering' a lot to deepen your child's insights and projections and, ultimately, their capacity for healthy reflective functioning. Have some fun with this and roleplay it with your child. Tell them to do/ say something and watch for what expression you put on in response to them. When they see your expression they must guess what you are thinking and feeling. Now ask them what they could change about what they are doing/ saying to get your expression to change. Repeat this to allow for a range of responses to a range of behaviours.

....

15-minute practice: Active listening

It is important that you attune to your child in other ways by using your active listening skills. How do you know if you are actively listening or partially listening to your child? Add the quiz below to your parental self-audit and stay on top of it.

1. When your child is talking to you, do you stop what you are doing?

2. Do you give your child your full attention when they are talking?

3. Do you interrupt when your child is speaking?

4. Do you repeat what you think you heard your child say, just to be clear?

5. When your child is asking you about a problem, are you already thinking of the solution before they have finished speaking?

6. Do you fold your arms in front of you when you are upset or angry while listening to your child's explanations?

7. Do you look your child in the eye when they are speaking to you?

8. Do you ask questions to keep the conversation going or when you don't understand something your child is saying?

9. Do you offer other ways for your child to 'talk' to you, like playing together or drawing a picture of what happened?

10. Do you encourage your child to talk again later by telling them you are there to listen if they need you?

CHAPTER 4

Attachment

Attachment has been quite the buzzword in
parenting circles for many years now and has
even spawned its own attachment parenting
movement. Of course, what is known as
'attachment parenting' is not, in and of itself, a predictor
of secure attachment, but just another school of thought
around parenting.

But investing in your attachment relationship between
you and your child is something worth doing, worth
doing right and as early as you can. This is not going to
be an intense theoretical read on attachment theory but
I do want to introduce you to the concept and underpin
it with practical ways in which you can shine a light on
what works for you and your family, resulting in secure
attachment relationships. Here are some key points to
hold in mind as we explore attachment and discuss how
and when it develops in the parent–child relationship.

The infant's right brain begins to develop before the left
brain; in fact it begins to develop at the very beginning of
infancy. The right brain is the part of the brain that deals
with visual cues, sensory data, emotions and non-verbal
communication. It is the part of the brain that attachment
impacts on. The left brain is where language develops and

it does not, generally, begin to mature before the age of 18–24 months.

Attachment behaviours engaged in by the parent/caregiver serve to regulate (calm, soothe, stimulate, engage) the infant's right brain and the maturing limbic system contained therein. The limbic system is fundamentally associated with housing all our emotional functions. The purpose of developing a positive healthy attachment relationship with our children is that it ultimately supports them to develop that all-important capacity to self-regulate their own emotions.

INNER WORKING MODEL

The best parenting outcome is that we raise secure, healthy, kind and independent children who grow up to be able to separate from and live in the world independently of us. We introduce our children to the world and how to be in the world by how we relate to them and model ways for them to relate not only to themselves but also to others. The parent–child relationship is central in supporting children to develop what we call a positive inner working model (IWM) and healthy sense of self.

IWM is simply a term for how you view yourself, others and the world around you. A positive IWM looks something like this:

Self – I view myself as lovable, inherently good and deserving of good things.

Others – I view others as safe and trustworthy.

World – I view the world as a (generally) positive place where good things happen and it is safe for me to be out there.

A negative IWM will look more like this:

Self – I view myself as bad (not that I do bad things but that I am inherently bad as a person), unlovable and deserving of bad things.
Others – I view others as unsafe, untrustworthy and a threat to me.
World – I view the world as a scary and unsafe place where bad things happen.

An IWM is not something you can just present your child with; it is something that evolves gradually through calm, clear, consistent and predictable parenting responses, and its development begins in infancy.

It is worth reflecting on your own IWM because it is very difficult to grow a positive sense of self in a child if you are starting from a negative IWM in yourself. It is possible to move from a negative IWM to a positive one, but this takes specialised clinical support and you should consult a suitably qualified mental health professional if you feel you would like to discuss this.

STAGES OF ATTACHMENT

Forming a healthy attachment relationship is something that starts gradually and builds and strengthens as you and your child grow together in your relationship and knowledge of each other. It comes from that sense of *feeling felt* by another person, of *getting gotten* by someone else. This starts with our mother, includes our other parent and extended family circle and then others whom we bring into our lives as we grow and seek to repeat this sense of feeling felt and getting gotten by others.

We start this process in how we interact with, touch and meet the needs of our infants. Then, as we get to know each other more and more and fall more in love with our children, this attachment strengthens. From your child's perspective, this allows them to learn that their relationship with you can withstand those times when you might be angry with them because they know that you love them, and if they go away from you they trust you will welcome them back when they have calmed down. When they have a good sense of this aspect of your relationship, along with that important capacity for people permanence, they can confidently begin to move away from you and do their own thing while knowing you hold them in mind and they hold you in mind.

This phase of your child separating from you to explore and develop an identity independent of you is not easy for either parent or child and it is often a challenging time, but it is vital that your child learn to be an independent person. Repeating this process leads to them becoming a strong and resilient person in their own right, which enables them to try new things, take considered risks and learn from their mistakes. It also leads to them knowing that they can call upon you no matter what and they trust that you will be there for them.

Co-dependent stage

When a child is born their first stage of development is called the co-dependent stage of development, also known as the fourth trimester. This is when a baby does not yet know that they are a separate being from their mother and believes that they are one and the same person. When an infant gazes up at their mother's face, locking their gaze with her eyes, they do not see their mother but themselves reflected in her. Simply put, when you look at your child with love they do not see you but rather see themselves as lovable. And repeated experiences of this connection with you will reinforce this emerging sense of self as lovable and deserving of love. When they begin to separate from this emotionally intense relationship with their mother after approximately four months of age they will seek to repeat the emotional experience they have had with their mothers. (Of course, this is not to say that fathers or other parents are not very important to infants – they are. A child's other parent is also a key attachment relationship in their early life and this bond between the baby and their other parent should be invested in just as much from earliest infancy. The other parent also serves an essential function at this stage in caring for the mother so that she is as available as the baby needs her to be. She cannot be so available without this support and help.) This means they will actively seek out people who make them feel as lovable as she did. So when an acquaintance looks at your child and smiles and admires them, but of course doesn't actually *love* them, your child will be less interested in them than they are in family members who do truly love them and thus reinforce the sense of self that is already developing in them.

What's vital is our ability as parents to consistently, predictably and reliably meet our children's physical and emotional needs and to do so with joy and warmth. This, combined with our children's ability to receive this care from us, to avail of what we make available to them and to draw benefit from it, contributes to the strength or weakness of the attachment relationship. This is why it is impossible to 'spoil' a newborn baby. All attachment research asserts that the more you respond to their cries in these early months, the less needy they become as they grow up. Touch them, hold them and respond to them as much as you can to reduce distress and lower their cortisol levels. When they know that you will meet their needs, they trust you, and trust is the first developmental milestone. Developing the capacity to trust is the aim and task of the first year of life. If babies learn to trust during this period, their brains are wired to trust throughout life.

Cycle one: 0–12 months

Following the co-dependent stage of development is attachment cycle one (0–12 months), which is all about a child having their needs met and developing a capacity for trust in others. The baby has needs (to be fed, to be changed, to be picked up, etc.) and they indicate their need the only way they can, which is by crying. The parent/caregiver then responds appropriately to this need and soothes the baby, allowing trust to develop in their relationship. Now, through repeated experiences of this cycle in the first year of life, the baby learns that when they have a need they can cry and anticipate with certainty that you will meet their need and help them to feel better. They trust in you and in their connection with you. In this manner, trust is actually the first developmental milestone for children.

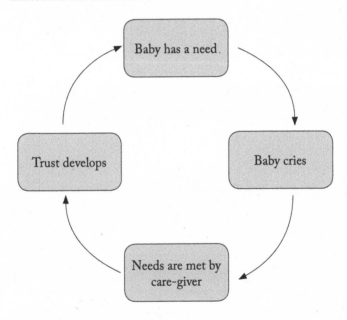

If for whatever reason this first year attachment cycle does not go as well as this, we see different outcomes. This is in no way a judgement – sometimes life happens to people and they may, for various reasons, be unable to respond consistently to their young baby's needs. I believe that most people are doing the very best that they can when it comes to parenting. And remember, repair and recovery are always possible, so even a rocky start can get back on course with some specialised therapeutic support.

But if you cannot negotiate this first attachment cycle with your baby in a healthy manner it will look more like this:

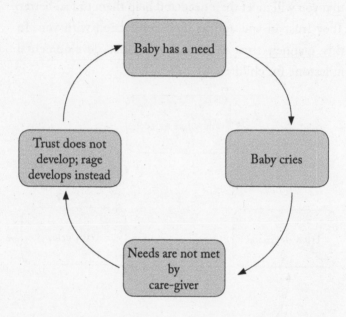

In this instance the caregiver does not respond appropriately to their baby's cries, or perhaps responds inconsistently to them, which makes it difficult for the baby to trust their parent to meet their needs. Where trust does not develop, we see rage develop in its place. A baby will either turn this rage inwards and will emotionally shut down, appearing flat, disengaged, even depressed; or they will turn it outwards and become overtly angry, shouting, thrashing, etc. This would be considered a rupture in the young child's attachment formation and you will need support from a professional to repair it, though it is reparable.

Cycle two: 12–24 months

For the purpose of this chapter, let's assume that the first year attachment cycle went well and trust has started to develop in your relationship with your baby. Now they can progress to attachment cycle two. Once you have met their needs, they will hit you with their wants. While this stage is often referred to as the 'terrible twos', this behaviour is actually developmentally very appropriate – it's just not always pleasant to parent through. This cycle looks like this:

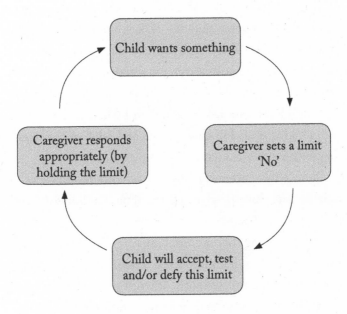

Here the young child wants something; let's say ice cream. You say, 'No, we're not having ice cream, we're eating our dinner.' Now your child will accept (unlikely), test or defy this limit. In other words, they will respond by getting louder and perhaps physical. They will shout and throw a tantrum: 'I WANT ICE CREAM!!' So far, so normal …

I did say it wasn't pleasant to parent through, though. It is what happens next that will make or break this cycle. When your child yells and tests/defies your limit you must, gently yet firmly, hold the boundary by repeating, 'I said no ice cream, now let's eat our dinner.' In doing so, you teach your child that it is okay for them to want something, but it is not up to them if they get it or not – it is up to the safe, trusted, loving adult in charge, in whom they have already built trust from attachment cycle one.

If, however, you give in each time and when they get louder you acquiesce and say, 'Okay, fine; have the ice cream. Just stop screaming!', you also teach them a lesson. You teach them that screaming is a very effective form of communication and that when you say 'No' what you really mean is 'Just scream louder and then I will say yes', which your child will do, loud and proud, and often at the most inopportune public moments possible.

Now, take a moment and exhale because absolutely nobody gets this one right all the time. I'm going to say that again ... *absolutely nobody gets this one right all the time.* If you are reading this and thinking you nail this one every time, you should definitely write a book, develop an app and retire on it. But seriously, when it comes to this one, focus on getting it mostly right most of the time because good enough is good enough. Toddlers have incredible stamina and they can go on much longer and more loudly than we can, so learn the value of picking your battles. If that means caving in and buying the packet of sweets when it all kicks off in the supermarket, just so you can get the shop done and the child safely back into the car seat (we have all been there), rest assured that you have not derailed your child's emotional development by doing so. Just try to establish and hold your boundaries as best you can as much as you can and this will get the job done.

It is only by going through this second year secure attachment cycle that children will ever be able to learn to accept limits on their behaviour. Indeed, it is by going through these two attachment cycles – the healthy attachment cycle in the first year and then the second year secure attachment cycle – that children learn to trust, engage in reciprocity and regulate their emotions. It is then that they start to develop a conscience, self-esteem, a capacity to develop empathy, and the foundations for logical and critical thinking are laid down.

Permanence: 12-18 months

Running between these two cycles are object and people permanence (12–18 months old). Permanence is critical to developing a secure and healthy attachment. It starts with object permanence. Think about when you wave a teddy in front of your child's face and then quickly conceal it behind your back, saying, 'Where's teddy gone?' and just as quickly returning teddy, declaring, 'Oh, there's teddy!' and then repeating this – to the delight of your child. From the small child's point of view, when teddy disappears he ceases to exist and it is therefore magical and delightful when he suddenly reappears. One day, through repeated experience of this type of play, the child will peek behind your back and see that teddy has not disappeared and actually still exists even when they cannot see him.

It's similar to a child sitting in a high chair who throws their spoon on the floor. You pick it up, only for them to toss it back onto the floor, squealing in delight while you lose the will to live as you repeatedly pick it up again. This may be tiresome for parents but it is amazing for the small child because, from their perspective, when the spoon disappears, just like teddy did, it ceases to exist and when it magically reappears their little mind is blown. Of course, they need to test this out by doing it over and over and over and over … until the time comes that they lean over the side of the high chair and see that the spoon is on the floor and it's not magic at all that it reappears because it never actually disappeared. By doing things like this, a child develops object permanence and once they have that, they can turn their focus to developing people permanence.

Initially, when you leave a room and they can no longer see you, you cease to exist, and when you return they are relieved and thrilled all at once. They will show you this by flapping their arms, squealing and reaching out to you. If you have had a baby, you know the drama of trying to get to the toilet or the shower. You use your disembodied voice to reassure your baby that 'mummy/daddy is just on the toilet and will be back in a minute', but at this stage hearing your voice when they can't see you is not enough to reassure them and they continue to squeal for you. So now you bring them in their bouncer to the bathroom with you and you leave the door open, conceding that privacy in the bathroom is a thing of the past – at least until they acquire people permanence. Then the bathroom and its closed door can be a five-minute sanctuary. Am I right?

But we can prepare our children for separation through play – concealment and discovery play, otherwise known as 'hide and seek' or 'peek-a-boo'. You hide behind your hands ever so briefly and then reappear with a soft 'boo' and a smile as you catch their gaze and reconnect before hiding again. Repetition of you disappearing and reappearing prepares your young child to cope with you not being there. They have developed trust that you will be there to meet their needs through attachment cycle one and this helps them to trust that if you go you will return to meet their needs. As they get used to you going and returning they are able to hold you in mind and feel held in mind by you. This is referred to as *constancy*. Constancy means that your child can *feel* your love and the safety, comfort and joy that they experience when they are with you, even when you are separated. In other words, they can hold you in mind and feel held in your mind when you are apart. In healthy attachment relationships, children can also experience this state of constancy when you are angry, frustrated or disappointed in them. They understand that your love is constant even when you and/or they are showing negative feelings and the associated behaviours that go with these feelings.

Attachment play

Play can help solidify each of these stages of attachment. When it comes to playing with infants, it is important to strike that balance between stimulating and over-stimulating them. Many people are surprised that *play* is something that very young infants do. But we are playing with our children from the very beginning of their lives, or at least we need to be. The language of play here is **relationship play**. When you think of 'play', your mind probably goes to toys, games, imagination and creativity. But at this early stage of infancy, it is all about relationship play.

At the very beginning, from the moment of birth, infants are submerged into a bath of language and sensation. Their optimal viewing distance is 6–12 inches, which is why we all naturally tend to lean in towards the face of a new-born. Babies show a preference for their mother's face from the first few hours of life. By two to three months old they show preference for her eyes above all else and can pick out their mother's eyes from anyone else's. For a baby, the safe and trusted adult who loves them is the focus of their play and the type of play you are engaging your baby in is about **touch, eye contact, mirroring, sounds, rhythm** and **song**. You will be counting their piggy-toes, softly rubbing noses with them, gently tickling, blowing onto their tummies to make fart noises, pretending to eat them or chase them when they start moving on their own, clapping their hands for them until they can do it themselves and mirror you clapping yours as you sing a song. Babies want to look at and touch your face, stroke (pull) your hair, smile at you and have you smile back. This is the 'serve and return' function of early attachment. From your baby's perspective, you send them a message and they send one back in response. This is how we connect. This is relationship play and it comes before toys enter the picture. You will find that returning to this person-to-person interactive type of play, even when your child is older, will be helpful and enjoyable for them, especially if you are experiencing any difficulties in your relationship with your child. It is always good to return to a time when your relationship was strong and good and reconnect at that level.

Relationship play also relies on good use of **prosody**. Prosody refers to elements of speech – pitch, pace, pause, intonation and volume. People who are good at using their voices to expressively engage someone can convey a sense that they are not only following but are really interested in what the other person is saying. This is a good communication skill in general but is especially useful when it comes to 'talking' with your baby or young child who is still learning how to speak. When you talk to your baby about your plans for the day together and they 'coo' or 'ga-ga' back to you and you then respond as though they have understood what you are saying, your baby will completely engage with you and turn to look up at you, delighting in the 'conversation' you are having. For example, I might say to my baby, 'We're going downstairs to have breakfast and then we'll go out for a walk. Would you like that?' and the baby might make a sound, to which I will respond, 'Oh, you're right, baby, we'll need our coats and hats today because it is very cold. Where would you like to walk today?', and when the baby again makes a sound I will interpret it for her and say, 'Well, then, the beach it is, and we'll see the water and some doggies out for a walk, and what else will we see?' Baby mumbles and I reply, 'Yes, the swans! I forgot all about the swans. We'll see if they are around today too.' And so on.

This is something you will do dozens of times every day when you are with your baby and while it (hopefully) feels effortless and normal, something you do without much thought, it is a very different experience from your baby's perspective. This process of prosody or using the elements of speech and your voice to connect with others has its roots in the early parent–infant relationship and underpins our attachment relationship with our children. Babies are biologically predisposed to attune and respond to higher-pitched, lilting tones. This type of voice gets a baby's attention and can have a calming, soothing and emotionally organising effect. Equally, loud or gruff, static, monotonous voices are difficult for babies to connect with and their attention will drift. This is also why you find yourself singing your actions aloud to your baby: 'We're going to change your nappy, your nappy, your nappy. We're going to change your nappy, all the way upstairs.' (I'm betting you sang that in some kind of tune as you read it.)

This is why *you* are, and will always be, the best 'toy' your young child can have. These moments of meeting, shared joy and serve-and-return interactions help to develop a positive inner working model and a securely attached, healthy sense of self in your child that will stand to them throughout their life as they continue to grow and develop.

....

15-minute practice: Attachment

Sing personalised lullabies: pick any lullaby or even nursery rhyme you might know but add your child's name, features or interests into it. For example:

- 'Twinkle, twinkle little star, what a special girl you are, hair so fair and soft pink cheeks, big, blue eyes from which you peek, twinkle, twinkle little star, what a special girl you are.'
- 'My Jamie lies over the ocean, my Jamie lies over the sea, my Jamie lies over the ocean, oh bring back my Jamie to me.'
- 'This little piggy likes dinosaurs, this little piggy likes chicken and chips, this little piggy likes playing outside, this little piggy likes singing songs and this little piggy likes stories and cuddles before bed.'

Row, Row, Row Your Boat: Sit on the floor with your two-year-old or put a younger child up onto your knee. Holding their hands (arms outstretched), row forward and backwards as you hold their gaze and sing, 'Row, row, row your boat, gently down the stream, merrily, merrily, merrily, merrily, Lucy is a dream.' This activity supports trust. Your child has to trust you won't let them go when you push them backwards. There is also a brief disconnect followed quickly by a reconnection when you break eye contact and find each other again. Finally, the rhythm is soothing and regulating for young children.

Peek-a-boo: Playing Peek-a-boo supports the stage of permanence. Bring your child's hands up to cover their own eyes and say, 'Where is Susie, where is Susie gone?' and quickly bring their hands back down so you can delight in finding them. Then, hide your eyes and say, 'Where is Mummy/Daddy gone?' and quickly reappear. Encourage your child to mirror you and to hide their own eyes as they get closer to the age of one and onwards.

Let's dance: Pick them up and simply waltz around the room humming or singing as you swing around and move in/out.

Read together: It is never too early or too soon to introduce books and reading together is a lovely calm way to come together. Pick books with bright but not too busy illustrations. Talk about what you see in the pictures as well as the words and encourage your child as they grow to do the same.

....

ADULT ATTACHMENT

Bear in mind that our attachments are dynamic and evolving rather than fixed or static. They grow, change and adapt as we grow, change and adapt. This growth and development is an essential part of raising children and results in them internalising the strength and durability of their relationship with you. The attachment relationship between a child and their parents will serve as the foundation stone for our relationships in adult life because adult intimate relationships and close friendships follow these same consistent and predictable steps. How many times have you thought, 'I just want to meet someone who gets me,' or 'I love this person, they get me'? Don't we all want that in our close friendships and intimate adult relationships? Well, that desire has its roots in the early infant–parent attachment relationship. The attachment we form with our parents in infancy leaves a mnemic memory trace, like a breadcrumb trail, and we seek to repeat and reinforce it as we come into contact with other people throughout our lives. So while the first attachment relationship is a crucial one, it is certainly not our only one.

I want to add a thought here for anyone who may be reading this and reflecting on an early attachment relationship that was less than ideal, either the one you had with your own parent or the one you feel you have had with your child. While our own attachment patterns are very important when it comes to building an attachment relationship with our children, it is very important to remember that *attachment can be healed*. It is never too late to engage in a process of repair and recovery when it comes to a ruptured attachment. You will not achieve this alone, so do reach out to a skilled professional who can support you in this process. There are various types of attachment therapy, but if it involves your attachment with your child it should be a joint parent–child approach such as theraplay (www.theraplay.org) or dyadic developmental psychotherapy (www.ddpnetwork.org).

It is true to say that there is no better way to discover what unprocessed issues we have than to become a parent. Having children will bring your 'issues' screaming to the surface. This is no reflection on you or the kind of parent you are; it is just part of the journey that led you to where you are.

CHAPTER 5

Play is the Language of Children

There is a wealth of neuroscientific research showing that access to spontaneous free play has an important, indeed essential, role in developing strong physical and mental health in children, the benefits of which continue throughout our lives right up to old age. Access to this spontaneous and free play, and having playful relationships (with both peers and attachment figures), are the foundation stone on which children develop social competence, emotional resilience and a capacity for emotional self-regulation, as well as the life skills and flexibility necessary to adapt to, respond to and deal with unpredictability, stress and risk throughout their lives.

You might be thinking that our own parents didn't seem to put much conscious thought or effort into how we all played as children, but times have changed, as has our physical and social environment. Raising children now is quite different from what it was just one or two generations ago. Many children spend a lot of their week in structured care environments where the opportunity for spontaneous free play is restricted by supervision and environmental restraints. Of course, they get to play while they are in daycare, but 'free play' is often shoe-horned into designated times and built around a more structured pre-school curriculum. The urbanisation of our society means that it is not as easy for children to simply get outside to explore and play; instead, they are taken to supervised play centres or playgrounds.

Smart devices have changed the landscape of how children play – and not for the better. Children are now playing in a more insular, sedentary manner than in previous generations. And there is an impact on their motor skill development (both fine and gross) as well as their capacity for creative and imaginative thinking. If screen-based devices are a part of how your children play, try to ensure that they are only a small part. Try also to ensure that you can delay the point of access to screen-based device play for as long as you can, and certainly limit it until they are over seven years old, have negotiated the three stages of developmental play and are better placed to self-regulate their emotional arousal (very important given how hyper-stimulating screen-based play can be for many children).

STAGES OF PLAY

Being a child means being small in a very big world. This can be overwhelming and frustrating. Very young children are entirely dependent upon their caregivers for everything, even their movements around their home. They take their lead from us and are highly attuned to how we are feeling and even what we are doing. They seek out our gaze and attention a lot, looking for us to validate and praise what they are doing, to delight in them, to encourage them and at times to join in with them. This is why we cannot look upon those blissful moments when our young babies crawl away to explore the play mat alone as time for us to reach for our phones. This is a time for us to observe what they are doing and when they look up they should find our gaze upon them and not into our screens. In infancy and into toddlerhood, our young children are very curious. They thrive on explorative play such as opening and emptying all the drawers and presses in your home. By encouraging this curiosity and helping them to try small things for themselves they begin to feel more competent and it doesn't take them long to want to do more and more for themselves. By the age of four years, children strongly desire independence while simultaneously feeling quite powerless in the enormous world around them. This leads to frustration and a sense of failure at not being able to do the things they want to. It is also by the age of four that they develop greater awareness of moral reasoning, which is why you start to hear endless declarations of 'It isn't fair!' Spontaneous and free play affords children the control they crave but cannot have in their day-to-day lives. Children's play is essentially tied up with various states of power and control. It is how they begin to develop a sense of autonomous agency. Through playing, children are exploring their social and physical power in relation to both the world around them and the other children in it. Play is about pushing boundaries, testing limits, imagining what it would be like to be in charge, to be the grown-up who gets to tell others what to do.

In play, a child gets to be the architect of their own world, designing it as they want it to be and assigning roles to others they might be playing with. This process exposes and introduces them to what it means to be in control and equally what it means to be out of control. This playful engagement and exploration of themselves, others and the world around them empowers them to take chances, take risks and push themselves further. The magical and imaginative world of play offers a new landscape to a child that is quite different from their real-life world. In this play landscape it is not only possible but allowed to exert control over others, to push boundaries, to be in charge and to allow oneself to be out of control in a way that is not acceptable in the real world. There is both order and disorder in the world of play. Children can experience conflict, combat, negotiation and reconciliation, all within one play. They can play independently and collaboratively. They can play in a sensory and motor manner just as easily as they play games that have rules (often rules they have created themselves). They can play with objects (toys) and in a more symbolic way (either without objects or by repurposing a stick/rock/flower to represent something else entirely). Play allows them to develop their own ideas and understand what it is to have fun and be silly.

I believe that play is the most important aspect of our children's childhood. It is how they learn about themselves, others and the world around them. It is how they process and make sense of their experiences. It is through play that they integrate new learning, develop understanding, draw conclusions and work out resolutions. Through play, they make connections and develop important attachment relationships with people in their lives. Play enables them to develop an emotional vocabulary and learn the art of emotional self-regulation. If we want to gain insight into and better understand our children and their world, we must learn their language.

We must learn how to play and, moreover, to play at their developmental level. There are three stages of developmental play that take a child from birth to seven years old.

Embodiment play: 0-4 years

Stage one of developmental play is a stage of sensory and messy play. This is about skin-to-skin touch, singing, dancing, clapping, sand, water, Play-Doh, finger painting and music and rhythm. You should be able to tell by looking at the child what they have been playing with – it will be all over them. This stage of play is about containment and learning that they have a skin that contains them and understanding where they end and the world around them begins. This stage of play will take the child from infancy to three and a half to four years of age.

This type of play is important and pleasurable for most children. There will be some who have some tactile sensitivity and find messy play unpleasant. There will also be parents who dread this type of play and the mess that it brings with it. Messy play is not in everyone's comfort zone, I know this, but it is very important that you find a way to get comfortable with it, as our children need to experience it. One way to get comfortable is to contain it. Here are some ways you can do this.

- **Use a tray/drop cloth/bib/jacket**: Get a food tray and place it on the floor or on a table top. Tell your child that this is where the messy play stays (be sensible and put a plastic bin bag or a wipeable oilcloth underneath). Now you can spray shaving foam and perhaps mix in some glitter and/or food dye drops on the tray for your child to mix with their fingers and make patterns with. Keep some older clothes that you don't mind getting messy. Call these their messy play clothes and have them put them on before the activity begins.

- **Make it disposable**: Take a few minutes to wrap the table (whether it's your kitchen table or a child-sized play table) with paper. You can use a roll of drawing paper or wallpaper lining. Wrap the table and Sellotape the paper underneath the table top so that it is all covered. Lay out lots of messy play items – paints, glue sticks, scraps of paper, etc. – and let them paint and colour and make a mess all over the table. When they are done simply unwrap your table with everything still on it and throw it all out together.

- **Structure the messy activity**: This will give you more control over messy play. Consider putting sensory basins on the floor together, e.g. get four washing-up bowls and put sand in one, dry/crunchy leaves in another, paint in a third and water in the fourth. Lay out some paper between basins three and four. Have a soft towel beside number four. Have your child walk through each basin in order, so that they feel the sand between their toes, then the crunch of leaves, then step into paint and make footprints on the paper you have rolled out, then the basin of water, which cleans their feet and you have your soft towel ready to dry them. Consider having some lotion to rub into their feet, and fresh socks too. Perhaps also seize the opportunity to play 'This little piggy' on their toes and/or hold their little foot up against the palm of your hand and measure their foot, exclaiming at how much they have grown and how their foot is almost the size of your hand.

....

15-minute practice: Embodiment play

Sensory basins offer a wealth of benefits for children. Engaging in sensory experiences like running fingers through rice grains, through shaving foam sprayed onto a tray, or through pouring water can distract and calm a child who is feeling over-stimulated or anxious. It promotes self-discovery and encourages a child to explore new textures, which in turn supports social and emotional development. Offering textures like dried beans, sand or cotton balls promotes hand-eye co-ordination and gives the opportunity for a child to pinch and grasp, enhancing their fine motor skills. As children discover new textures and objects, they tend to have a verbal response. Engaging them in a sensory basin is also a great way to work on language development. These basins can be either wet or dry. A wet sensory basin involves taking a large plastic bowl or sink basin and half-filling it with tepid water, then adding glitter, washing-up liquid or even some spices. For a dry sensory basin you can use dry, uncooked lentils, beans and pasta. Just plunging little hands into the bowl and feeling the textures is a lovely sensory activity.

Singing games like 'Head, shoulders, knees and toes', 'The hokey-pokey' or 'When you're happy and you know it clap your hands' promote whole body movement and balance while teaching children to follow directions and focus their attention.

Offering plenty of options for **free play** is important too. When given pavement chalk and outdoor equipment like balls and hula-hoops, children will engage their fine and gross motor skills without even realising it.

Music (rhythm- and synchrony-based activities) activates every subsystem in the brain, including areas that regulate emotion and motivation. Setting aside time to make music together allows children to bond with family members and gives them a sense of containment. Music time can be especially beneficial to young children, even when they are non-verbal. For them, music can be a way of expressing themselves and interacting with their peers.

Provide children with instruments such as egg shakers, bells or toy drums. You can make your own instruments: pour dried peas into an empty Pringles tube and Sellotape the lid on (decorate the tube or wrap it in colourful paper) to make a shaker; or stretch a burst balloon over an empty baby formula container (without the lid) and secure it in place to make a great finger drum. Encourage them to make noise with their instruments and move their bodies to the music. Sing songs that incorporate the name of each child so that everyone feels like they have an individual role in the activity, e.g. 'James is here today, James is here today, Clap our hands and shout "Hooray!" that James is here today' and repeat for everyone's name ... even if there are just two of you doing it.

Additionally, incorporate music in other activities of the day. Sing songs while cleaning up and transitioning into new activities like nap or snack time, for example, 'We are clearing up our toys, we are clearing up our toys, it's fun to sing and make some noise while clearing up our toys.'

Projective play: 4–5½ years

Stage two play is about story and narrative. In projective play the child uses toys to show increased awareness of the world outside themselves. This stage will take them from three and a half to four years old up to five or five and a half. Six months either side doesn't make a huge difference, as long as they do it. Here we see an increased focus on stories and narrations to further explore and investigate objects, people and their general environment at a deeper level. They are responding to the world outside the body. When children use toys to introduce possible scenarios or friends, the representation of multiple perspectives occurs naturally. Taking on different roles allows children the unique opportunity to learn social skills such as communication, critical thinking, turn-taking, winning/ losing, solution-focused thinking, problem-solving, general civility and empathy.

You know what this looks like. It's when your child picks up two (or more) toys (cars/trains/teddies/dolls/ figurines) and has them talk to each other. To do this type of play, a child must be able to consider a situation from two or more perspectives at the same time. This is the root of developing a capacity for empathy. Often the situation they play out is one that is relevant to their own lives. For example, they might have one toy say, 'It's time to go to bed,' then the other replies, 'But I'm not tired and I need a drink.' Then the first might respond, 'Now is not time for a drink, now it is time to sleep,' and so on. In other words, things that they experience in day-to-day life get projected outwards, outside themselves and onto the toys, and they process the experience in this way. Finger puppets are great at this stage of play, but they will use any two toys. If you draw two eyes and a mouth on each index finger they will have them talk to each other, or if you're out in a restaurant they will make the salt and pepper pots talk to each other.

Children play and create stories like this in a natural way and rarely need interference from parents. They might invite you into this small world; if they do, play with them, but let them lead. If your child has not or did not do much of this type of play, it is never too late to go back and close this gap with them by introducing the play yourself. You might even start a story and hand them the toys to finish it, then you take one character while they take the other; do this for a short time each day, gradually adding time onto it and then stepping back once they get it for themselves.

This is a vital stage of play, given the social skills it supports, but it is often the stage of play that we are getting most wrong. This is, I believe, because it is also the age we are most likely to give children a screen-based device to occupy and/or distract them. Screens sabotage this stage of play, short-circuiting natural development and catapulting the child forward without having successfully negotiated these crucial life skills. Watching cartoon characters play and interact on a screen is not the same as having the toys in their hands play out the story they are imagining. One activity keeps a child cognitively and virtually engaged; the other has them in their body, in the moment, using their own imagination and processing their own experiences.

The writer Philip Pullman has often spoken of the importance of stories in children's development. He said, 'Thou Shalt Not is soon forgotten, but Once Upon a Time is forever', and 'There are some themes, some subjects, too large for adult fiction; they can only be dealt with adequately in a children's book.' There's a story to match pretty much any life crisis known to a child, so invest in stories and really nurture this stage of projective play for and with your child.

....

15-minute practice: Projective play

Think of the times we are most likely to hand our children screens to occupy them: car journeys, in cafés and restaurants. But how about putting a couple of **finger puppets** or small toys in your pocket/handbag and using those when the need to distract and occupy occurs?

You may recall **fold-over stories** from your own schooldays. Take a sheet of paper and write the first line and a half of a story. Fold down the top line of the page and hand it to your child. They write a line and half following on from what you have written, fold down their first line and hand it back to you. Continue until you are at the end of the page and then unfold and read aloud the story you have created together. This is fun but also allows us time to connect and attune to each other's cues.

Bedtime stories are a great way to give your child an appreciation of narrative play. A 2012 article in the *Irish Examiner* reported that out of 300 parents interviewed, 60% said that increased work pressure meant they were 'too busy to read their child a bedtime story'.

Children really need this time with their parents and reading a bedtime story has been linked to improved literacy, creativity and better sleep. A bedtime story and reading or storytelling with your children are vital to their development. Stories also have a positive and significant impact in a child's developing brain.

But storytelling is not just about books. Consider using **story sacks**. You can buy these online but of course you can make your own at home easily and a lot more cheaply too. A story sack is a large cloth bag (or an old pillow case) containing a child's favourite book with supporting materials to stimulate language activities and make reading a memorable and enjoyable experience. While you read or tell the story you can play it out and/or talk about your favourite bits. For example, a story sack for the 'Three Little Pigs' would contain the following:

- A copy of the story
- Models of the three pigs and the wolf
- Some straw, some twigs and some stones or pebbles
- A non-fiction book about buildings
- Prop(s), e.g. a toy hammer or hard hat
- Paper and crayons.

You can adapt this for any book you want to use in your story sack.

Something children love to hear is **your stories**. The story of how they were born (not the biology but the narrative around it – who drove you to the hospital, who first called to meet them, what songs you first sang to them, how you chose their name). They also love to hear stories about you when you were their age and about other members of the extended family.

There's a nice tool for achieving this connection with your children. It is called the **Do You Know Scale**.[3] I think it's a good idea to sit and ask/answer these of yourself and see how much you know about your own family before you start doing it with your child. And, of course, don't sit them down *Mastermind*-style and grill them, but gradually interweave these stories into what you tell them over time, bit by bit. However, it is not really the *content* of your family history that is important but the *process* by which it is known/shared/talked about. The best way to share and hear family stories involves everyone sitting down, feeling connected to each other, without distractions.

The Do You Know questions are:

1. Do you know how your parents met?
2. Do you know where your mother grew up?
3. Do you know where your father grew up?
4. Do you know where some of your grandparents grew up?
5. Do you know where some of your grandparents met?
6. Do you know where your parents were married?
7. Do you know what went on when you were being born?
8. Do you know the source of your name?
9. Do you know some things about what happened when your brothers or sisters were being born?
10. Do you know which person in your family you look most like?
11. Do you know which person in the family you act most like?
12. Do you know some of the illnesses and injuries that your parents experienced when they were younger?
13. Do you know some of the lessons that your parents learned from good or bad experiences?
14. Do you know some things that happened to your mother or father when they were at school?
15. Do you know the national background of your family (Irish, English, German, South African, etc.)?

16. Do you know some of the jobs that your parents had when they were young?

17. Do you know some awards that your parents received when they were young?

18. Do you know the names of the schools that your mum went to?

19. Do you know the names of the schools that your dad went to?

20. Do you know about a relative whose face 'froze' in a grumpy position because he or she did not smile enough?*

* This last question is here to remind us that not everything our families tell us is absolutely true! The nature of storytelling is that the narrative shifts and changes as it is passed on. Interestingly, 20% of respondents in the original DYK research answered yes to question 20 ... go figure!

Another technique (suitable for any age over 4 years old) that is traditionally therapeutic in its application but can be easily and pleasurably used at home by you and your child is **six-part story making**.[4] Every story/movie plot can be broken down into six essential parts.

1. A main character (not necessarily human – ask them to name the character and draw something that shows if they are indoors or outdoors)

2. A task for the main character (to go somewhere, do something, find something, become something)

3. Things/people who get in the way of the main character achieving their task

4.   Things/people who help the main character achieve their task

5.   The main drama of the story (its high-tension moment)

6.   How it ends (it can end happily ever after, but it doesn't have to).

For this story technique take a sheet of paper and draw six boxes on the page. Invite your child to draw something for each of the above steps in each of the boxes. When they've finished, turn over the page and, starting with the words 'Once upon a time' (because anything is possible in Once upon a time), they must write out their story. If this is too difficult for them, they can speak it while you write it out. When they've finished they say 'The End' and you read their story back to them so that they get to hear their own words. This is a creative and imaginative way to break a story down into its separate parts. It also helps you see how your child might overcome challenges and utilise supports, how they work through drama and tension to bring about a conclusion or outcome of some sort.

....

Roleplay: 5½–7 years old

The third and final stage of developmental play is roleplay. This is not to be confused with *dress-up* – that lovely play your children do with costumes (Disney princess dresses, Bob the Builder costumes, etc.) – because when a child dresses like Elsa from *Frozen*, they are playing out that story we have all seen far too many times. There is nothing wrong with dress-up play, but it cannot take the place of roleplay. If I hand a child my scarf it can be a magic carpet taking them and their teddies far, far away on an adventure, or a picnic blanket that they and their toys sit on, or a sling to bandage their arm as they play at being injured, or a cape that can make them a superhero ... In 'costume dress-up', the prop decides what the play is, but in *true* roleplay, the play decides what the prop is. Think old school when it comes to building up your roleplay box and use scarves, old shirts, handbags, shoes, hats, etc.

This third stage of play takes a child from five/five and a half right up to seven years old. Here they are not projecting roles onto their toys but instead inserting themselves into the role so that they are the mummy/daddy/doctor/nurse/vet/teacher, etc. Everything they took in in stage one and projected outwards in stage two allows them to insert themselves into the role now. You will see evidence of both stage one and stage two play here as they further explore their world and develop their sense of self.

This stage of play is dramatic and you see this when the child roleplays at being the teacher and has the teddies lined up against the wall while roaring abuse or assigning lots of homework to them. You might hear this and wonder what on earth is going on in that school and feel compelled to go see the teacher, but fear not – this is dramatic play and they are testing out how big and bad they could be if they were in this role.

Children use this stage of play to restructure/rearrange aspects of their life events to gain a better understanding of themselves and the world around them. This is where the row you think you had in private last night is getting played out verbatim in the play room with the child from next door in a game of mammies and daddies. This is when we all become increasingly aware of how our children learn by mirroring us and are soaking up everything, good and bad.

Children will often bring their siblings into this type of play, assigning roles as they direct the play itself. They may even invite you into their roleplay and, if and when you can, it is a great experience to enter this imaginative world with them. Remember to stick to the role that they assign you, follow their direction and let them lead the play. When the play is done, or perhaps you need to exit the play to attend to something else, be clear about 'de-roleing'. In other words, be clear that you are no longer the evil witch's prisoner, you are now mum or dad again. You are all leaving the world of imagination and re-entering the real world.

I appreciate that this may be difficult for busy parents, so remember that good enough is good enough. If this type of parent–child connecting doesn't come naturally to you, fear not – here is a cheat sheet step-by-step guide to get you there.

....

15-minute practice: Roleplay

Start with **availability and time**. Set aside 15–30 minutes and show that you mean business by turning off phones, disconnecting the doorbell (or at least hanging a DO NOT DISTURB sign on the door) and dressing appropriately for sitting comfortably on the floor. This lets your child know that you are fully present, in the moment and engaged with them and them alone.

Design a **play space.** Take a large blanket (a double bed duvet cover is also ideal) and spread it on the floor. This will be your play space for the duration of the playtime together. Now you need your play toolkit. Plan ahead for this and ensure that you have some art supplies, including finger paints and Play-Doh for messy play, some figurines for narrative and projective play and some roleplay props. You can put each into three of the four corners of the play space. Now allow your child to choose something else to include in the play space to fill the final corner.

Remember, you are in your child's play world as a **follower, not a leader**. Don't give in to an urge to take over. Let your child guide you and reinforce their endeavours and creativity by praising *effort over outcome*. Try using phrases like 'You worked really hard on that picture', 'I can see you took time to choose the colours', 'You went really slowly to make sure those blocks could stand on top of each other', etc. If your child does defer to you and ask what you should play together, encourage them to choose by saying, 'You decide – what would be your favourite thing out of everything on our play mat to start with?'

Structure is still the parent's job, and you can achieve this by following your child's lead as much as possible but stepping in when necessary to hold a boundary, such as 'We don't put Play-Doh on the floor, we use the tray instead.' It will also be your responsibility to watch the time and manage it with and for your child. At the start you can say, 'We will have 15/20/30 minutes of playtime together and I will be in charge of the time. A bell will ring when we have five minutes left, again when we have two minutes left and then the third bell means we are done for today and I will tidy up our blanket and you can choose something to keep playing by yourself.' Time is an abstract notion for children, so structuring it like this allows them to feel the time going past and the end coming. Or you could use a 15-minute sand timer and say, 'When all the sand hits the bottom our playtime together will end for today and I will have to go back to doing some jobs.'

Connectivity through play is about quality rather than quantity; so don't worry if you feel you can only manage one such play session a week. It is better to do this once a week every week than three times a week one week and then not again for three months. Consistency and predictability are key to authentic connection.

....

EMOTIONAL REGULATION

It is only by going through these three stages of play – embodiment, projective and roleplay – and having these consistent moments of meeting with you through play that your child will learn to self-regulate their emotions. Until they can do this for themselves they co-regulate with us, their parents and caregivers. What this means is that if your child is losing their temper (and they will, of course, from time to time) and they manage to get you to lose your temper with them, they will be unable to co-regulate with your rage and will further escalate.

When this happens, acknowledge to yourself that you have lost this round, take a minute to try to get calm and emotionally regulate yourself, and simply manage the situation until your child is calmer. If, however, when they lose it you can stay calmer (you'll never stay 100% calm – if you could you should bottle that strategy and sell it!) they can downward regulate with you. In this way, you are serving the function of a thermostat, not a thermometer[5], in that you are controlling and managing the heat of the situation rather than simply measuring and matching it.

DIMENSION PLAY

In addition to being able to co-regulate your child upwards or downwards as required it also helps you to have some insight into the different regulating dimensions inherent in parent–child play so that you know what type of play you need to reach for in different emotional temperatures. When you are using dimension play you are taking a more active lead than in the designated 15-minute playtime detailed above. However, you should never have to say that you are in charge; as soon as you have to say you are in charge you really aren't. So we don't say it, we do it and we lead in a kind, connected, more collaborative way with our child.

When your child is using acting-out behaviour and/or you notice their mood and behaviour pattern changing, stop and quickly assess what response might they need you to communicate back to them in order to reassure them and help them co-regulate with you, back to that optimum arousal level. As always, rule out the chance that they might be physically dysregulated by asking yourself if they could be unwell, hungry, thirsty or tired. Respond to their physical state first, as this might resolve the behaviour in and of itself, while recognising that it is very difficult to emotionally co-regulate when you are physically dysregulated.

Sometimes our children need us to help them to organise their feelings and to make sense of what they are feeling; sometimes they just want to enjoy and be enjoyed by us; sometimes they want us to be gentle and mind them as though they were younger and sometimes they want us to challenge and push them a bit. Understanding that our children need different things from us at different times is important but so too is understanding what type of play corresponds with those different needs. These can be broken into four separate dimensions: structure, engagement, nurture and challenge.[6]

- **Structure** communicates to your child: 'There is someone who is bigger and wiser and kind looking out for you; you can relax.'
- **Engagement** communicates to your child: 'You are not alone' and 'I like being with you.'
- **Nurture** communicates to your child: 'You are worthy of good care.'
- **Challenge** communicates to your child: 'Wow, look what you can do!'

Structure

The purpose of structuring activities is to organise and regulate your child's experiences. As the adult, you set limits, define bodily boundaries, keep your child safe and help them to complete sequences of activities. Here we focus on you being in charge as a means of strengthening your child's sense of reassurance, safety, creation of order, emotional co-regulation. As our children gradually learn to be in control of themselves, this kind of play assures them of a sense of order while addressing any sense of inner and outer disorder they might experience.

15-minute practice: Structure

Hand-stack: Sit opposite and facing your child, as close to eye level as you can. You start by providing the base hand and ask them to put their hand on yours, then you put your other hand onto their hand and they put their other hand onto yours. You continue taking turns as your hands go upwards. When your hands block your child's eyes, you can say, 'Oh, I can't see you, where have you gone? Oh, there you are!' Once you have stretched as high as your child can reach, pause and then come back down. Younger children may find this difficult to co-ordinate so you can say, 'We tumble down,' once their hands have reached as far as they can. With more impulsive children, you may find that you have to hold on to their hand, only releasing it when it is their turn to move; or you can co-regulate their impulsivity by saying, 'My turn, your turn, my turn, your turn.' Very young children might do better using fists rather than hands as they will get up/down more quickly. Older children who don't want to 'hold your hand' may like a variation such as finger stack, just using the tip of your index finger, or a floating hand-stack where you get your hands as close as possible without actually touching, but you still go up/down.

Mirroring: Here you invite your child to act as your mirror and to (non-verbally) copy your actions. You can sit/kneel and make these small actions, or for younger children or children who need to move about more, you can stand up and have them copy bigger movements. You always start doing the actions for them to copy, but you can then allow them to do three or four actions for you to act as their mirror and follow their lead.

Engagement

The purpose of engaging activities is to connect with our children in a playful, positive way. We want to create opportunities to enjoy our child and for them to feel enjoyed by us. In this type of play, you provide excitement, surprise and stimulation that is tuned into your child's energy levels so that you make sure that they do not become over- or under-stimulated by the activity. While playfulness can be part of any interaction, it is clearly an important factor in engaging children in joyful shared interactions. It says, 'You are fun to be with and I enjoy being with you.'

....

15-minute practice: Engagement

A sailor went to sea: Sit opposite but facing your child at their eye level. Using a rhythm activity like this (you can use a rhyme of your choice), clap your own hands and then each other's in sequence, doing three claps on each other's hands when you get to 'sea, sea, sea' or 'see, see, see': 'A sailor went to sea, sea, sea, To see what he could see, see, see, And all that he could see, see, see, Was the bottom of the deep blue sea, sea, sea.' As you both gain competence and confidence, go as fast as you can and then as slow as you can using the different speeds to regulate your child upwards or downwards.

Four-part handshake: This is a good one if your child is a little anxious at the point of separation when you are leaving them to school/day care. You start a special handshake with one move (a normal handshake) and ask your child to add on the next part (a hand slap, for example), then practise the two parts together before you add a third part (maybe a fist bump) and practise all three parts together before your child adds a fourth part (something like a high five); now practise the four parts in a row a number of times until you know you can remember it.

....

Nurture

Nurture activities are soothing, calming, quieting and reassuring, such as rocking, feeding, cuddling and holding. These activities make the world seem safe, predictable, warm and secure. Healthy parent–child connectivity enables a warm, tender, soothing, calming and comforting relationship. The message of nurturing care is, 'You are lovable. I will respond to your needs for care, affection and praise.'

....

15-minute practice: Nurture

Texture guessing game: Sitting opposite your child, rub a feather across their cheek and then do the same with a cotton ball so they can feel the difference. Now invite them to close their eyes and alternate between stroking their cheek with the cotton ball and the feather. If your child cannot keep their eyes closed, then suggest they keep their eyes open while turning their head to one side. If your child doesn't like to have their face touched, you can stroke their arm or the back of their hand instead. And as I have come to learn with many parents over the years, if you do not like the feeling of cotton wool, simply use two different material textures of your choosing (i.e. tissue paper or a silky scarf or fluffy pom-pom). Accuracy is not important here, so it doesn't matter if they guess correctly or not. What matters is that they can sit still and stay connected with you. So avoid saying 'right' or 'wrong' and simply say 'that's good guessing'.

Cotton ball touch: Again you will sit opposite your child and invite them to close their eyes. Touch somewhere on their body (a knuckle, a finger, nose, a cheek, a shoulder, a knee, etc.) and your child, without peeking, must name the part you have touched.

....

Challenge

These are activities that help children to extend themselves a little bit and are appropriate to the child's level of functioning. Challenge activities also allow children to take appropriate risks and master tension. Healthy parent–child challenge play encourages children to move ahead, to strive a bit more, and to become more independent while stimulating development, encouraging progress, setting appropriate expectations and taking pleasure in your child's achievement. The message is 'You are capable of growing and of making a positive impact on the world.' The type of play I encourage here is not only mindful of your child's developmental capacity (we want to ensure mastery so only set challenges they can achieve and then gradually build on these) but is also more collaborative challenge rather than competitive challenge.

15-minute practice: Challenge

Thumb wrestle: Sitting opposite and facing your child at their eye level, take their right hand in your right hand and curl your fingers together, leaving your thumbs raised. Say, 'One, two, three, four, I declare a thumb war. Five, six, seven, eight, try to keep your thumb straight,' and then you push your thumbs against each other while holding hands. Whoever holds the other's thumb down for three seconds wins that round. Repeat this with left hands and then cross both your arms at the same time and do a double war. Watch your competitive streak here! We are aiming to boost your child's confidence and sense of mastery over a task, so they should win at least two out of three rounds. To increase the challenge with older children, consider applying lotion to each other's hands and then do it with slippy hands!

Newspaper punch and paper basketball: Stand or kneel, facing your child. Ask them to stand and, moving only their arm, take a practice punch into the air (specify into the *air* so that you don't get punched!). You do this to see with what kind of strength and from what direction the punch will be coming. Then take a sheet of newspaper (tabloid size works best for little hands, but be aware of the content on the page you use – sports pages are good) and hold it out and away from your body. On your cue, they punch as hard as they can into the middle of the page you are holding taut. With any luck they will punch right through it, splitting the page into two pieces. Repeat with each of these pieces so that you have four pieces. Remark on how strong they are and they might even let you check their strong muscles. Now roll each piece into a ball. Move a little further away and make a circle with your arms to make a basketball hoop. They can toss the paper balls into the hoop, one at a time. Increase the challenge (if they are able for it) by making the arm hoop smaller or slowly moving it side to side or moving yourself further away.

....

CHAPTER 6

Playing as Parents and Family Time

Parents make children, but our children make us parents. We have to invest in this parent–child relationship as much as we can, as early as we can and for as long as we can. Organising outings and nice days out or family board games are all lovely ways to spend time together as a family. But playing together every day is cheaper, easier and a lot more impactful. Therapeutic parent–child play is a special way of spending time together that uses the shared joy and playful connection created between you and your child to bring you physically and emotionally closer to one another. These types of activity involve physical closeness to one another, a lot of eye contact and touch. They are about having fun and enjoying each other. Most of all, they are easy to do and do not involve expensive toys or props but basic things you have lying around the house.

Most of these activities can be played with children of all abilities, but go with what you know your child is developmentally capable of. You can adapt many of them to suit your child's developmental needs.

It is important that we adults know and recognise when to step back and leave children be and when to step in and engage in their world with them. If your child proactively invites you to play with them they are letting you know that they want to connect with you and the easiest way for them to do this is at their level. If we cannot accept the invitation immediately, it is still important to acknowledge it. 'Thank you for inviting me to play with you. I would love to. I have some adult jobs I have to take care of first but as soon as I am done we can play together for a while before dinner/bedtime.' But if we are distracted and we miss the invitation altogether, we have missed the opportunity for a moment of meeting between our child and us.

When our children seek us out for a connection, they are letting us know that there is something they need and that they believe the answer is connection with us. Perhaps they are holding onto an uncomfortable experience from school or with friends that day and it is unsettling them; they instinctively know that connecting with us will help them to process the experience and co-regulate with us to a more comfortable level. If they do not get to do this, that discomfort will likely build and find its way out in a more negative, destructive, acting-out type of behaviour. This is why I tend to interpret children's negative acting-out behaviours as a need for connection rather than a demand for attention.

RELEARNING PLAY

Our children love to play with us because they love to connect with us. But it's usually been quite a while since we adults lived in a world of imagination and play, so our play skills might be a little rusty. I remember a mum who came to see me saying that her six-year-old son kept asking her to play cars with him and she didn't know how. This may sound unusual, but perhaps if you have grown up in an all-female/all-male household, if you work in an area that requires you to be up in your head all day, if you didn't get to spend much time with children until you had your own, if you didn't get to play much yourself as a child, it is entirely possible that playing with boy/girl children or playing in general may seem like a foreign language to you.

I reminded her that she lives with an expert in playing with cars and it would be perfectly okay to defer to his expertise and have him show her how to play with cars. What he really wanted was to connect with her, be in the moment with her and bring her out of her head and into his world of play with him.

A dad came to see me with his five-year-old son. We were going back to close some early sensory/messy play gaps in this child's development. Dad arrived on day one straight from work and wearing a very expensive suit. He did not look ready to sit on the floor with us and get messy, but that was our plan, so I went ahead and took out the lotion and the powder. You can imagine the state of this suit by the end of the session. I never saw that suit again but I did see a dad who arrived with a change of outfit each session and this, in turn, signified something special to the little boy. When dad changed into his 'play clothes', as the child called them, it communicated to him that his dad was here and ready to play, to get messy, to have fun, to connect with him.

I include these stories to highlight how sensitive our children are to the subtle messages we may not even know that we are communicating to them. If we feel we do not know how to play with them or that we are not really available to enter their world with them, even by what we wear (a work suit or a skirt and high heels that make it impossible to sit comfortably on the floor), they pick up on these cues and they feel disconnected from us.

The last thing I want to do is make you feel that playing with your child is yet another task you have to fit into your already packed and demanding day. I don't want you to feel bad if you do not like playing with your children. Many parents did not get a lot of positive play experiences when they were children; some feel that because they haven't played since they were young children they don't know how. This is about finding easy and fun ways to connect with each other as a family using the language of play while being practical and finding ways to embed the play into your existing routine. Stick with me: this is entirely possible, I promise you!

'What if I don't like playing with my child?' When I hear this question I always wonder if what you really mean is, 'I don't like playing and it makes me uncomfortable and embarrassed.' So it's not that you don't like playing with your child – you just don't like playing at all. This is where your parental self-audit proves invaluable. Where does your discomfort with play come from? Did you have enough opportunities to play as a child? Did you play alone or with others? Do you ever remember your parents playing with you? Perhaps you have internalised that play is kids' stuff and adults have no business being in that world. Or perhaps it is so long since you have played that you are out of practice. Or perhaps entering into the world of children and the world of play where you make-believe, dress up, put on voices, pretend to be a baby, etc., is awkward, embarrassing and way out of your comfort zone. Understanding our relationship with play is an important part of understanding our block to playing with our children. It is not that you don't love your children and spending time with them, it is that you are uncomfortable with this imaginary, sensory, often unstructured way of being. And there is a reason for that.

Children, especially young children, tend not to say, 'I've had a hard day and I'd like to sit and talk it through with you.' They are far more likely to say, 'Will you play with me?' as a means of processing their hard day. If play is difficult for you I suggest you take the approach detailed later in this chapter of child-focused but parent-led play – this approach offers more structure, which will make it easier for you to play. Always start with an activity that you feel relaxed about playing, as children will pick up whether or not you really want to play with them. Play as a language is about doing, not thinking and talking, and often the thought or idea of sitting and playing and getting messy and silly is far worse than actually doing it is. Often parents who have been blocked to play find that they really enjoyed the experience of doing it and found it a lot easier to relax and laugh and be in the moment than they had imagined they would. This is largely because of how contagious a joyful child can be and how quickly we can get lost in those moments of shared joy with our children. That is what playing with our children is all about. It is an opportunity to experience a moment of meeting (pure connectivity) and shared joy (emotional synchrony).

There are two ways to use the language of play to connect with each other. One is to take a child-led approach; the other is a more child-focused but parent-led approach. I fully appreciate the demands of any parent's busy day, and since we follow the rules of good enough being good enough, 15 minutes of play a day, perhaps aiming for 30 minutes each weekend day, is all you need to do.

CHILD-LED PLAY

Ideally, include all family members, or as many as you can gather together. Parents join children on the floor and do so in a curious and interested way: 'What are you playing? Do you think I could join in for a while?' I say 'for a while' because you probably can't sit there all afternoon (if you can, that's great). Remember, in this approach you are following your child's lead, so let them assign you a role in the play and allow them to lead the direction, tone, pace and theme of the play. This approach allows you to enter their world of imagination and meet them where they are. This can be helpful when you feel that you do not really know how to play because, guess what? Your child is an expert in play and they can teach you how to do it.

15-minute practice: Child-led play

A good way to show your child that you are truly present with them is to **turn your phone off**.

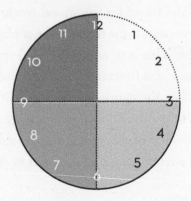

Tell them how much **time you have to play** with them, but remember that time is an abstract notion to children, so make it understandable: 'I have 15 minutes to play with you. That is when all the sand in our timer hits the bottom.' Or consider using a colour-coded clock. You can make this by taking a cheap, plastic clock and popping the front cover off it. Colour in the segments on the clock. For example, 15 minutes' worth is coded blue. You can use the colour-coded clock system for bedtime or homework also. Colour the required time segment in different colours, e.g., if blue is for play, choose green for homework and purple for bedtime. Explain 'When the big hand is in the blue part we can play together' or 'When the big hand is in the red part we all sit at the dinner table'.

Now sit **physically close** together but allow them space to move around. Focus all your attention on your child and what they are doing.

If your child tells you that the egg box they took from the kitchen is a spaceship, it is a spaceship. In other words, allow your child to **identify the toys** in the play.

Use your voice to reflect the intensity and tempo of your child's play by saying something like 'Oh, the cars are going really, really fast!' in a fast, higher-pitched voice, or 'Your car is hiding hoping mine doesn't find you,' in a gentle, low whisper.

You can also **reflect orally** what you see them doing. For example, 'I can see you're being so careful placing those blocks on top of each other to make a tower. You really don't want them to fall.' Or if said tower falls and your child kicks out at the blocks, rather than reprimanding them, help them to process the feeling by saying something like 'You're disappointed that your tower fell and you feel angry at those blocks for not doing what you wanted them to. Let's try it again together and see how high we can make it.'

While you will not reprimand your child during playtime, it is perfectly okay to **set a boundary** around what kind of behaviours you are and are not comfortable with: 'I don't feel comfortable throwing this ball inside the house in case something gets broken or one of us gets hurt. Let's see if we can make paper balls that we can throw instead.'

Let your child know when your **play time is coming to an end**. They may accept this or they may struggle to accept it as they are having such a good time. Flag it by saying, 'The sand is nearly all gone so my playtime with you is coming to an end for today, but we'll do it again tomorrow and thank you for playing with me.' If this isn't enough, add, 'I know you'd like it if I could sit here all day and play together. That would be great fun but I have some jobs to do now.' It can be helpful to add a distraction line too: 'It's time to get a snack, come with me to the kitchen,' or 'Come outside and help me bring the washing in.'

....

PARENT-LED PLAY

When play is parent-led, that should be unspoken but clearly understood. If you have to say, 'I'm in charge,' you are not really in charge. You lead by *doing*, not *saying*. Parent-led play means that the play is structured and is a set of consciously selected activities that aim to help your child to regulate their physical and emotional self while reassuring them that you are there providing safety and taking care of them. Parent-led play should not involve a dictatorial or bossy style of parenting; it is about being playful and leading in a natural way.

Parent-led play is very much about the present moment. We do not refer to what happened yesterday or how your child should be behaving at some event coming up at the weekend. This is a right-here, right-now, in-the-moment playful connection between you and your child(ren).

Plan ahead and ensure you have the uninterrupted time and materials you need available and to hand so that you do not need to break the play connection to go and get something. Have the games you want to play in your mind, along with two spares should some of them not go to plan. Ensure the activities you have selected are suitable for everyone in your family to be able to play together.

What follows is a list of sample activities and games that you can use in this type of play. This list is not exhaustive and of course you can add your own in here too.

....

15-minute practice: Parent-led play

Balloon Tennis: Work together to keep a balloon in the air with each person hitting it when it is closest to them. Help each other by calling out the person's name when it is close to them. Make this more engaging by calling out a different body part that must be used to achieve this, e.g., 'Let's keep it up using just our fists/our palms/our pinkie fingers/our elbows,' etc. This is a more-the-merrier activity so more people means more fun and more excitement. If you are a very large family group or if some members are getting a little over-excited, consider structuring it more by passing the balloon in sequence around the circle rather than just up in general.

Hand-holding balloon tennis: Everyone in the circle holds hands and you work to keep the balloon up in the air without breaking your hold. This is good to keep excitable little ones more regulated and also introduces more touch if you have children who resist holding your hand at any other time.

Blanket-sway-balloon: Everyone stands in a circle and holds a piece of the blanket (or sheet). Place a balloon in the middle of the blanket and the parent in lead role calls out one name at a time. When someone's name is called, the rest of the family have to lift, dip, tilt their section of the blanket to send the balloon over to that person and do the same when the next person's name is called out. Repeat until everyone has had a go.

Blanket games: Take your blanket and have everyone sit in a circle with their shoes off and their feet stretched into the middle. Cover all feet with the blanket and have everyone wiggle and mix up their feet entwining around each other. Now each person takes a turn at (lightly) squeezing a person's toes over the blanket and trying to guess whose foot it is. Once guessed correctly, that person takes the next go and so on.

Cotton snowball fight: This is a very fun group/family activity. Everyone is given a pile of cotton balls and when the parent-in-charge says GO, each person pelts their snowballs at the others in the family. Everyone must freeze when you say STOP or do a countdown: 'Snowball fight ends in 5-4-3-2-1'. You can *manage impulsivity* by using a red light/green light system here – they can throw when you say GREEN LIGHT and must freeze when you say RED LIGHT. Keep repeating this in a stop/go approach.

And finally you can also use familiar sing-song activities here such as **Hokey-Pokey** or **Head, Shoulders, Knees and Toes**.

There are no ends to the types of games you can play here. I bet you will start to remember lots of great group games you played as children, and why not include some of those here too? The key is to know why you are playing one game over another and ensuring that you are holding the developmental capacity and needs of each family member in mind when you select your activities. Having fun together with these moments of shared joy is about connecting, being in the here and now and building memories that will last a lifetime. I'm willing to assert that no child will grow up saying, 'I remember the time I was allowed to play alone on my tablet,' but will definitely say, 'I remember that time we played a cotton ball snowball fight together and how we all laughed when the cotton ball got stuck in Mammy's hair.'

BEING PLAY-PREPARED

Being play-prepared empowers you to feel more in control and you will have a play toolkit that will help you parent through any eventualities. I want to emphasise the value of this type of play for you and your child, especially as it does not require spending money on expensive toys/props but relies upon you and some simple bits and pieces, most of which you will have at home already. You are not expected to be your child's entertainer – they do not need this from you – so pick and choose what you feel will work best for you and your children and stick to those.

On-the-go kit

Take 15 minutes to create an on-the-go kit. Sometimes you're delayed in a waiting room, have to wait for someone in a café longer than expected or have to hang around waiting to pick someone up. I have a Ziploc freezer bag that I carry with me that contains enough items to keep children engaged, stimulated and occupied without having to resort to a screen-based device. This play-on-the-go kit fits easily into a coat pocket or handbag or the glove box in your car.

The kit should contain items such as:

- 1 double sheet of newspaper (this allows you to play newspaper punch and basketball).
- 1 small party bag-size bottle of bubbles (for playing bubble pop, bubble tennis).
- 2 finger puppets (you can tell a story to your child, have them interact with you or give them to them to play at their own story).
- 1 feather.
- 2 straws.
- 3 cotton balls (you can play cotton ball/feather guessing game, cotton ball touch, cotton ball face massage, feather blow, cotton ball hockey on a coffee table).
- 1 sheet tinfoil folded up (unfold it and make some body part moulds of your child – fist, hand, foot, nose, etc.)
- 1 generous strip of toilet paper (play toilet paper bust out, karate chop, even snowball fight with the squares rolled up).

- Lotion (for hand massage, slippy thumb wrestle, to care for adventure marks).
- 2 strawberry laces or a fruit winder pack (use these to measure parts of your child, like their listening ears or their wiggly fingers, then feed the piece to them).
- Stickers (for sticker match).
- Temporary tattoo (you can keep a child very engaged while doing nice nurture-based touch applying the tattoo).

Having these items on hand will allow you to play almost all of the games mentioned in this book. This will all fit into a freezer bag, but you could also have a smaller kit.

Car journeys

These are simple and effective games that you can play while driving the car. They will keep your children engaged and calm without distracting the driver. These games require no props, so once you familiarise yourself with them you are good to go.

Jelly & ice cream: This is a great game to co-regulate your child passengers when you are on the move. Every time you say 'Jelly' they must respond with 'Ice cream'. But they must say it in the same tone you do, so when you whisper *jelly* they must whisper *ice cream* and when you yell JELLY! they must yell ICE CREAM! If you use a croaky voice or an up/down voice they must copy it. It doesn't really matter if they say jelly instead of ice cream – accuracy isn't the aim of the activity, engagement and co-regulation are. You want them to engage with you so they do not fight with each other (or do not get agitated by being alone in the back seat) and you are using your voice to co-regulate them, so if they are heightened you start loud and bring it down quietly.

Alphabet names: Take your child's name and use each letter to say something positive about them, e.g. CARA = Cool Adventurous Responsible Adorable. If your child is old enough, have them do one for MUM, DAD, GRAN, etc.

Seated Simon says: You call out the actions and they do them in their car seats. This means keeping it to small movements they can do sitting down, such as 'touch your nose', 'put your hands on your head', 'rub your tummy', 'clap your hands', etc.

Animal noises: You call out different animals and your child/children must make the noise of that animal. You can elaborate on this by asking them to also say what each animal's favourite food is.

PARENTAL STAMINA

Parental stamina is a term I use to describe that drive that somehow keeps us all going as parents. It's also a good tool for checking in with ourselves to see where our energy and focus levels are at on a given day or at a given time of a given day. Sometimes we will have a sense that we do not have it in us to be our most playfully engaging and connected parent selves. Our efforts to playfully engage or directly play with our children will be lacklustre at best, and of course those are the days when our children seem to demand even more of us. Though perhaps it is not a case of them demanding more on these days but more that we experience their regular level of demand as particularly overwhelming when we are running on empty. I've often heard parenting described as a marathon, not a sprint, but I don't really relate to this analogy because even a marathon ends after 26.2 gruelling miles and you get to have a hot bath and a rest so that you can recuperate and recover.

Parenting is a 24/7 engagement role and it can be hard to build in that all-important time for your self-care. It makes perfect sense that some days your parental stamina levels are low and it's all you can do to provide good functional care to your children (ensure that they are fed, dressed and safe), never mind crawl around the floor playing with them. Fear not, I have play solutions for these days too.

Planning for a **nurture afternoon** might be one such solution. This is when you make a quick and easy snack, bring the duvets down from the beds, snuggle on the sofa and watch a movie together while eating/feeding each other the popcorn/snack you made.

You could spend 10–15 minutes setting up and **building a fort** for your children using a blanket, cushions, chairs and the sofa and then let your children play in their new fort while you step back and have a cup of tea or read a chapter of a book.

Perhaps have a **spa day** – take a bowl of warm soapy water to soak little hands or feet, a soft fluffy towel to wrap and dry them in and some lovely lotion to massage into their skin.

Armchair play is another option when your parental stamina is lagging. These are games to play that allow you to sit in an armchair while your child gets to be active. A secondary gain from this kind of play is that you may well pick up on their energy and end up being more active than you thought possible at the outset.

Balloon volleyball involves you sitting down and hitting a balloon to your child who must hit it back to you. Bring a challenge element into this by keeping count of the number of volleys before the balloon hits the ground.

If you have a child who gets tired of armchair play quicker than you, consider turning it into a game of **wriggle worm** – tell your child that you are going to hold onto them (not too tightly or they will buck to free themselves and risk falling) while they wriggle free of your hold. Put up mild resistance so that have to really get their wriggle on but then let them loose and ask if they can wriggle all around the room, behind the sofa and all the way back to your lap as a worm.

You get to sit in your armchair while you set your child tasks and **time them**. 'I wonder how long it will take you to run from here to the kitchen, out of the back door, twice around the garden and back in through the kitchen to me?'

Create **a scavenger hunt** – take a few minutes to create a map or clues and plant them around your house with a prize at the end. If you plan it right this should take up a good 45 minutes to an hour. It might be worthwhile to plan a couple of these ahead of time so you have them instantly to hand when your parental stamina suddenly dips, as that's not the easiest time to plan such an activity.

You could play some music and they have to **dance** to it. Vary the tunes you select, from fast to slow, and use a variety of musical genres, including songs they know and some they don't know. Perhaps create a playlist ahead of time so you have it ready to go when you need it. Mix it up a little by blending in **Silly Animals** so that when you call out an animal, not only must they dance but they must dance as they imagine this animal would. You haven't lived until you've seen an elephant dancing to classical music or hip-hop beats.

What am I thinking? You sit silently in your armchair and your child must try to guess what you are thinking or feeling by the expression on your face or your body language.

Sitting in your armchair with your child sitting opposite you, take turns to send each other **silent messages**. This can be done by making shapes/symbols with your hands (e.g. make a heart symbol) or blowing kisses that the other must catch, to using your face to express a range of emotions. You can also take some paper and a pencil and draw/write messages to each other and then fold the paper into paper aeroplanes and fly them over and back to each other.

Gather the children around you on the sofa and each of you takes turns in **making up a story**. If they are a little older take turns adding parts to the one story. Perhaps you can audio record this and play it back at the end so that everyone can hear how funny the story sounds. You can also have everyone select one favourite book and rotate reading each book aloud. Pause after each story to talk about what parts they would keep in or change if they were the writer.

When night-time arrives and your parental stamina is through the floor but somehow your child's stamina is still sky-high you might like to use **paradoxical play**. Giving them an outlet to release that energy, even though it might feel that you are stimulating them, will help tire them out and bring them to a calmer state so that they can sleep. Try holding them (if they are still small enough to do this) and swinging them towards the bed with 'A one, and a two, and a threeee' and finally throw/flop them onto their bed. The paradox comes in when you start to sing a quiet lullaby, but then suddenly you yell instructions: 'Stand up, jump on the bed, touch your toes, flap your arms, wiggle your fingers, stick out your tongue, make a funny face …' and then (in a gradually quieter voice) 'Sit on the bed, rub your nose, do a big stretch and yawn, lie down, stretch all your muscles out, curl up on your side, snuggle under your blanket', etc.

Create a **busy box** for each child ahead of time. The rule is that this box only gets pulled out in cases of low parental stamina; keeping what's in the box off limits most of the time makes it that bit more enticing and engaging when they do access it. Fill a shoebox or small basket with a lid with little bits and pieces. Perhaps some putty/moulding clay, a small Lego set, some cars, miniature dolls and toy animals, a music box, a container with coloured balls/marbles/buttons (be age aware and developmentally aware as these could be a choking hazard for small children), and other novelty bits like this. Remember, whatever is in the busy box should be *selected, not collected*, and think of what engages your child's focus. Everything in here should be something that supports solo play – the point is that you don't have to play with them.

Having a few different types of play/games at the back of your mind will usually cover all eventualities. Of course, it is good for children to have time to play independently of you and, indeed, on their own, but it is equally important that they have some (always aiming for that all-important 15 minutes a day) focused play time with you.

Dips in parental stamina are normal and to be expected. Reflect on what else might be contributing to this in your life. Perhaps you are stressed or distracted due to something else. Be good and kind to yourself. Give yourself time to process and recover your normal level of stamina. However, if you find this state of low parental stamina is lingering beyond a few days and you cannot easily connect it to a specific and transient event in your life, you may need to consider a visit to your GP to ensure that you are physically well. If it turns out to be more of an emotional matter, consider booking in with a suitably qualified and accredited psychotherapist who is best placed to support you in identifying, working through and moving past such matters.

CHAPTER 7

Whining, Dawdling and the Value of Being Bored

'I'm bored.' Two words parents hear all the time, yet these two words can panic us into making sure our child is occupied, stimulated and amused. But boredom has a developmental value. It helps them to develop and express a desire of their own and this is essential in engaging their capacity to self-organise and regulate. The capacity to be bored is a developmental milestone for children and to achieve this milestone the child needs their parent to hold the experience with them and not get drawn into sabotaging it with distraction.

I wonder when we lost the inherent value of experiencing periods of boredom in our lives. Certainly the rise of smartphones and their pervasiveness in our lives means that we have less and less opportunity to be bored. Even when we're sitting on a bus or train on our daily commute we're constantly looking down at our phones, mindlessly scrolling and exposing ourselves to a constant stream of white noise of news, chat, images and video. We are shutting boredom out of our lives and out of the lives of our children and perhaps this seems like a good thing. Isn't it better that we and our children are active, stimulated and engaged? Yes, these are very important things in our lives, but to truly be engaged and present in our activities we also need time to do nothing, to sit and be, to think and allow thoughts just to float freely in and out of our minds as we process and assimilate all the learning and experiences we are exposed to every day.

If we can let go of our phones ourselves, we're often handing them to our children to keep them entertained and constantly engaged. We rarely afford our children or ourselves the privilege of being bored any more. Boredom helps children to develop the ability to amuse and entertain themselves and is an essential component of engaging their capacity to self-regulate as they grow. As we have already discussed, children under seven years of age do not self-regulate their emotions; they co-regulate in response to their parents/carers. To become self-regulating, children need exposure to an environment that will suggest things without imposing them, one that will not pre-empt their desire by force-feeding them with distractions and things to do, but one that allows them the time and opportunity to explore their surroundings and themselves.

It is essential that children are afforded the space and opportunity to be bored so that they can develop this capacity within themselves. When they have nothing immediately at hand, they will find something they want to do and experience and explore.

It can be revealing what a child's boredom evokes in us adults. We may hear it as a demand or even an accusation that we have failed or disappointed as a parent and this will affect how we respond to the child's state of boredom. We will either get angry with the child for being bored or we will jump to entertain and distract them to eliminate the boredom. It is a damaging, albeit unconscious, assertion of adults that a child should be interested rather than find what interests them. Boredom is the process of taking your time to find out what interests and motivates you. We must allow children to be bored.

Children's lives are increasingly becoming micro-managed by their parents and I believe this is coming from a parent's own desire to be the best possible parent they can be. But sometimes sitting beside you doing absolutely nothing means absolutely everything to your child.

Children certainly benefit from having extracurricular interests, but they do not need to be rushed from one activity to another. If the active part of their day is too long, children become hyper-stimulated, overwhelmed and overwrought; and lacking the emotional language to articulate this, they will revert to the language they do have and express this behaviourally, acting out to show you their internal chaos. Over-scheduling is an obstacle to self-organisation on two levels: first, it prevents boredom emerging; second, it blocks the development of creativity.

Creative children will always find a desire from within their boredom, they will occupy themselves and self-stimulate. Creativity is about self-expression, it is about trying new things and new ways of being and each and every child is capable of being creative in some area. Creativity is about challenging, exploring, questioning and playing with new ideas and ways of thinking. There are multiple benefits of integrating creativity into your parenting strategies, not least of which is raising independent, open-minded, curious, emotionally articulate and self-organising children. This is what flourishing is all about and don't we all want children to flourish?

FIDGETING

Fidgeting is another behaviour trait that I hear a lot about in my work so I was intrigued at the phenomenon of fidget spinners in early 2017. These were flat, plastic toys designed to spin in a user's hand. While they became extremely popular in early 2017 they have existed since the early 1990s.

Fidgeting is generally seen as a response to either anxiety or boredom. It tends to be something we do mindlessly while thinking or worrying about something or simply trying to work out a solution to a task at hand. Think of how we use paper clips, stress balls and rubber bands, even executive toys – if not to enable fidgeting, what purpose do they serve?

The reasons we fidget are mostly speculative – the area is under-studied – but it seems that if something we are engaged in is not interesting enough to sustain our focus, the additional sensorimotor input provided by fidgeting with an object that is stimulating, interesting or entertaining allows our brains a break from the boredom of the task at hand. This is certainly a distraction but distraction is not always a bad thing and a break like this can allow us to re-engage with what we're doing. This is 'floating attention' – the part of the brain that is bored is distracted by the fidgeting but allows the other parts of the brain to focus on the activity we are participating in. This is a pro-social benefit to fidgeting and used in this way it can serve a useful function.

Children who have a diagnosis of ADHD or other cognitive or sensory impairments tend to be more successful in an activity if they are able to control their body and movements. Fidget spinners can provide vital sensory stimulus for such children so that they can remain in a classroom or group setting longer and enjoy more time with their peers without getting so dysregulated that they have to be removed from the classroom.

However, not all children require additional or supported sensory input and these fidget toys can over-stimulate a child and certainly become a negative distraction, which is why I imagine so many schools banned them in the classroom. We must remember the importance of boredom in all our lives, but especially the lives of our developing children who, without boredom, will struggle to develop a desire or sense of what they like to do.

Having quiet, calm downtime is an important part of our day and we should avoid the urge to stay stimulated 24/7, as the brain needs time to rest and recharge. Remember that we can give our brains a break without using a gadget. Consider taking time to look out of a window and name the things we can see, or going for a short walk and taking in some fresh air, and try to embrace the benefits of boredom without always needing to fidget our way out of it.

So the next time your child tells you that they are bored, congratulate them and tell them what an exciting opportunity they now have to come up with something to do!

WHINING

Aside from boredom and fidgeting, I find that whining is a trait in children designed to drive parents crazy, which is why I hear so much about it. Whining is designed to elicit a response because the louder and longer your child whines the more difficult you find it not to respond to them. How you respond teaches them whether or not this is an effective communication tool.

To prevent them whining, don't wait until your child is already agitated and distressed before you identify what they are feeling. For example, if you are doing something and your child is calling for your attention, acknowledge it quickly. 'I see you're looking for me to play with you now, and when I've finished this job I'm doing I will be straight in to you,' and then deliver on this – so if you are doing the dishes at the time do not move on to hoovering before going into them.

While you may feel tempted to shout 'Stop it!' when your child persists in their whining, try to remember that it comes from a sense of powerlessness and is a way that children can gain some degree of power over adults. Small children rely on adults to do everything for them and whining is one way of taking back some of this power and control – and it gets a response!

When your child is whining it is always good to rule out illness first and foremost; let's be honest, we all whine when we are unwell! Once you rule out illness, ask yourself if you have been busier and less available to your child recently. Has there been a change to their routine? Have they been getting enough sleep? These factors may explain, though not necessarily excuse, the whining, so it is also helpful to come down to their eye level, take their hands in yours and in a calm steady voice say something like, 'I don't like it when you whine but I know it's because you want something. Try asking for what you want in this way,' and give an example. This tells them what you expect from them instead of just focusing on what you don't want to hear.

Here are some tips for dealing with a whining child.

- Recognise your own limits. If you need to walk away for five minutes, do that.
- Keep your face and tone calm and consistent and as neutral as you can. Come down to your child's eye level and try to get some skin-to-skin contact such as holding their hands in yours when you talk to them. This way you have a better chance of reaching them and of them feeling 'heard' by you.
- Spend 15 minutes a day playing with your child, doing something they like and that is at their developmental stage. Giving your child your presence over presents will help to minimise the whining.

⊕ Hold your boundaries regardless. 'Thank you for asking me so nicely to play with you, it makes me so happy to hear you use your good manners. Now it's time for bed and we will play tomorrow.'

DAWDLING

Any parent who has a child who dawdles knows first-hand how frustrating this can be, especially when you are trying to get your family from one place to another or from multiple places to one place and you really need everyone to stay engaged and keep up! However, getting frustrated with your dawdling child is one of the least effective things you could do in the situation.

Dawdling is one of the most common childhood problems and while it may seem as though your child is ignoring you, which of course is frustrating, this is not the case. The next time you hear yourself asking your child to tidy away their toys and get ready to go, for the second, third, perhaps even fourth time, stop yourself before you raise your voice and take a look at the scene. It is likely that your child is engrossed in an activity and is finding it difficult to transition out of it. Come down to their eye level and say, 'I see you're having lots of fun. Now it's time for us to go and collect your sister. Show me how you can tidy up and get your coat on and when you meet me at the door to go I will be smiling so big because I am so proud of your great listening.'

Dawdling is most common in young children, so remember that children under seven years old generally do not have the self-regulation or discipline to transition easily themselves. Becoming agitated and cross with them does not help because they will not associate your frustration with their dawdling; they will simply become anxious in response to your agitation. Instead, here are some ideas.

- Consider using a 15-minute sand timer in these instances. It allows your child to see the time they have left and wind down in a way an alarm or bell does not.
- Keep your cool, stay calm: explain, 'I have asked you twice, maybe you didn't hear me, but I need you to turn on your listening ears and put your toys away and get your coat right now.'
- Explain the consequences: 'If you don't get your toys put away and get your coat your sister will be waiting for us wondering where we are. I wonder how that would feel?' or 'If we are late you will miss your play time before school starts.'
- State step by step what you want your child to do. Be specific: 'Now it's time to get dressed, now it's time to brush our teeth.'
- Allow extra time: if your child takes longer to get going, build in extra time to your routine.
- Above all: reflect on your own relationship with time. Are you anxious when you are late? Are you rarely on time yourself? Be aware of how you can role model good and respectful timekeeping so that your child can learn from and mirror you.

Most children grow out of dawdling, but if it lingers as a characteristic beyond the age of seven it may well be a part of who they are, so parent them as they are and build in extra time when you are going somewhere, start tidy-up 15 minutes earlier and allow additional time to get where you are going

....

15-minute practice: Story stemming

While I am seeking to normalise what I very much understand to be challenging to all parents, I also have a therapeutic technique to share with you that could be very helpful here and in lots of other areas. This is the art of **story stemming**.

The kit you use for this should be stored in a Tupperware-type box and be used when you need it, rather than being integrated into your child's broader toy collection. You need to be able to find the pieces you want when you need them. You will need:

- A set of dolls/figurines – consider the Playmobil or Plan toy ranges. Make sure that you have a figure that represents everyone in your immediate family, along with grandparents and a few spare adult and child figures that can be used to represent friends, neighbours, teachers, etc.

- Dolls' house furniture – this is not absolutely necessary, but for younger children props such as dining table, chairs, TV, a bed, a toilet/bath/sink can help them picture the scene.

There are two ways to approach this technique and both will be useful at different times.

The first is this: You want to help your child know how they must **behave in certain situations** (how to use the bathroom; how to eat out at a restaurant; how to group play (birthday parties/play centres/activities etc.); how to share; how to travel; how to behave at school/pre-school, etc.).

Plan out your story ahead of time and practise playing it out with the characters. Have a clear beginning, middle and end to your story and keep it short and succinct – five minutes should be plenty. Play out the scenario *as you want it to happen*. In other words, show only the positive behaviour you wish to see from your child in this situation.

Tell them that you have a special story you want to tell them and that you will be using your special toys to tell this story. Sit at their level and remind them that their job is just to watch and listen to the story and only you will touch the dolls.

Play out the situation that you want to teach them using the dolls as the characters in the story. You can name one doll as your child in this story and use real names and specific places.

Repeat this story in the exact same way each day for five days (some children get it in three; others need seven to ten days, so use your parental instinct).

Now your child has something to default to when they are in this situation and perhaps getting hyper-aroused and beginning to act out. If they cannot default to the story you have played out by themselves, gently pull them aside and say, 'Remember the story we played? I want you to do it like that, please.'

The second way is to use a story to **find out more about your child's understanding** or way of thinking about certain situations. You will need the same kit as before and store it/introduce it in the same way, except this time you say, 'I'm going to tell the beginning of a story using my special toys and then you are going to show me how the story ends.' So this time they do get to touch the toys, but only when you hand the storytelling over to them.

Take a situation that has been recurring, such as sibling arguments or some trouble in the schoolyard that you don't have all of the details about.

You play out the beginning showing children playing happily together and after a minute or two you hand the dolls to your child, saying, 'Now you show me what happens next in this story,' and see where they bring the story. If the story moves towards catastrophe, don't interrupt to correct it but consider introducing a new element such as a teacher who walks over to ask what is happening and suggests a new way to play. Then hand the story back to your child and see how they integrate this new thread.

When the story is over, simply ask, 'And is that how this story ends?' and thank them for playing it out with you. Do not pass any further comment on the story.

You might decide to next employ the strategy mentioned above and play out the situation at hand for them, showing the positive behaviours, decisions and outcomes you wish to see happen.

Approaches like this enable you to connect with your child at their developmental level and to empower them to effect change in their thinking and feeling about situations that affect them from within. This will be much more helpful to your child in the long run than simply telling them what to do and how to behave or deal with situations.

CHAPTER 8

The Value of Magical Thinking

From the age of five years, children embrace magical and omnipotent thinking. This is where they believe in wish fulfilment – they believe that if they wish something it can happen. This includes wishing something negative about a sibling or parent they are angry with, and if that person falls or gets hurt, they can believe that their wish caused the injury and they are responsible for the outcome. This is also a time of being forgetful, absent-minded and appearing to be lost in their own little worlds, which may well be frustrating for us parents, but it is important that we understand this stage and step back to allow it to happen. What may be helpful here are some structuring techniques that enable you to keep the family schedule wheels turning without interfering with your child's magical development phase.

Perhaps you're thinking that this really doesn't sound anything like your child. So we'll also look at some ways in which you can introduce some of this magical thinking for your child.

DAYDREAMING

Let's start with daydreaming. I love daydreaming and if I could give every child a gift it would be the opportunity for more daydreaming. I believe that our best thinking occurs precisely when we allow our minds to wander. Indeed, a wandering mind is the brain's preferred resting mode, but these days we are so consumed with our gadgets and social media that we keep our minds permanently engaged and occupied and we are losing both the skill and the value of a wandering mind. Daydreaming or mind wandering offers our children many benefits. It allows us to better prepare for future scenarios, engage in self-reflection, consider a complex or challenging problem from other perspectives, create new ideas, come up with new games to play, and it generally allows the brain to recharge and reset itself so that it is ready to continue taking in new information and learning. In a daydream, nothing is ridiculous and everything is possible. Growing up kills daydreaming for most of us. Growing up demands focus, attention and being present in the now.

Our increased immersion in social media means that we demand more and more information to keep our brains constantly engaged and stimulated; we are bombarding our brains with visual information. When we are so busy gazing at the phones that are constantly in our hands we leave little opportunity to simply look out of the train or bus window and allow our minds to wander. We have forgotten how to just let our minds rest, but (most) children will do this very naturally *if* we let them. Albert Einstein was a well-known daydreamer (which didn't do his career trajectory any harm, now, did it?) and he once famously said, 'The intuitive mind is a sacred gift; the rational mind is a faithful servant. We have a society that honours the servant and has forgotten the gift.'

So what may look like inattentiveness or distraction or even idleness is actually a hub of creativity and the secret of re-setting a busy and overwrought brain. Rather than stopping our children daydreaming, we should be asking them to teach us how to do it. It is important that we not confuse true daydreaming, that unstructured space that enables our minds to wander between free thought and whatever memories might float in and out of our consciousness, with zoning out while playing a video game or glazing over while staring into a tablet device. These are very different and the latter actively sabotages any opportunity for the mind to wander, instead keeping the child's focus on the visual and cognitive stimulus of the screen. Feel free to interrupt *that*, but leave your daydreamers to their waking reverie.

So how do we protect and uphold our children's right and opportunity to daydream? Here are some ways to do it.

Lead by example. Get offline and turn your distraction devices off. Sit and simply be. Look out of the window and start by naming the things you can see, then the things you can hear, then the things you can smell, the things you could taste and the things you can touch. This sensory exercise will help ground you in the now and the world around you and then your mind is free to wander. Teach your children how to do this exercise if they struggle with it. This simple exercise to reset the brain is also very helpful if you spot that your child is getting over-stimulated and hyper-aroused and is a lot less confrontational than a time-out or being sent to one's room.

Ignore the protests of 'It's too cold' or 'There's nothing to do out here' – send your children **outdoors**. They can wrap up warm and there being nothing to do is precisely the point. Depending on age they could take a walk around your area or you can go with them and say that you will both just think while walking and can share what popped into your heads once you get home. You can also suggest drawing a picture of some of these thoughts at home.

Value daydreaming and talk about how wonderful it is to daydream and how it is as important as learning, studying, sleeping and playing. Explain that it is like yoga for our minds and because of that everyone in your family will find time to just let their mind wander each day.

Have your children spend **time in the garden**. If you are in a position to do so, assign them a little corner in which they can plant their own flowers and take care of them on their own. Gardening is a great opportunity to connect with the environment and quietly contemplate.

MAGICAL THINKING

Magical thinking is, for me, a rite of passage in childhood. A parent once called me in a fluster, concerned that she was lying to her children about Santa, the Tooth Fairy and the Easter Bunny. She felt she was telling her children not to lie but was lying to them. My advice was to keep lying on these topics because *if* we are to consider such traditions lies (and I'm not convinced that they should fall into that category), they are certainly *pro-social* lies whereby the benefits far outweigh the consequences. Children have a right to believe in magic and magical entities. Childhood is the only time in our lives when such things can truly exist for us and that window of childhood is small and getting smaller, so embrace it while it is there.

Magical thinking starts in toddlerhood when children believe that their thinking can influence the world outside of them; the time when food really does taste better to your child when it is in the blue bowl, not the green one. Young children are almost superstitious in their magical thinking and it can be part of what causes them to make outrageous demands as to who *must* put them to bed (perhaps they had a bad dream the last time mummy did it so daddy must now do all bedtimes in case the dream comes back) or what outfit they *have* to wear to pre-school (the last time they wore that superhero cape they got to have ice cream and pick the storybook that was read, so now they wear it over and over in the belief that it will bring about the same outcome). Rational thought is significantly underdeveloped in young children (not news to anyone with a toddler, I'm sure), so trying to reason them out of these beliefs can be futile and lead to heated behavioural explosions.

Magical thinking is a normal and healthy part of toddler and young child development. We do not want to end this stage prematurely, though we may need techniques to help keep routines on track as best we can if their magical thinking becomes a block. Consider meeting them at the level of magical thinking by presenting them with a magic spray (water with some lavender oil) in a spray bottle (the kind you get to put your shampoo into when going on holidays) and attach a formal-looking label that says 'Magic Sleep Spray'. Tell your child that this spray *always* makes children fall fast asleep and have the best dreams ever. Be supremely confident in how you assert this. Let them watch as you spray around their bed or lightly on their pillow. The aim is that they believe in the magic spray and are eager to go to bed to see what these amazing dreams will be. You can adapt your sleep spray for whatever unhelpful magical thinking you need to counteract.

Of course, magical thinking is not just for children. Folklore, old wives' tales, 'traditions', lighting candles, guardian angels (I've been known to call on my parking angels when circling a crowded car park searching for a space ... remembering to thank those parking angels when I get parked) and superstitions all continue into our adulthood psyche. More so for some than others, but it is fair to say that it is a part of human nature to look for patterns so that we can predict what will happen or believe that we can secure a particular outcome by following a set trajectory of actions. This is quite normal, healthy behaviour and betrays the fact that most people simply hate surprises and love being in control.

In times of extreme emotional stress we are even more likely to follow a line of 'magic-making' thought. There are some events in life that we simply cannot explain rationally and this is when we default back to the magical thinking of our childhood as we seek to make sense of something we cannot rationalise. Even if most of you doesn't believe, perhaps a part of you, even a very small part of you, does. And there is no better way to access that part of you that still believes than watching a child on Christmas morning. So embrace magical thinking, meet your child in their magical thinking as much as possible and remember, as Roald Dahl said, 'Those who don't believe in magic will never find it.'

Magic and imagination play an important role in helping children to understand the real world. This creative, magical, imaginative thinking time is actually helping to grow and develop your child's brain.

Young children often struggle to differentiate between fantasy and reality, between what happens in their imagination and what happens in the real world. This is quite normal for them and is developmentally appropriate. The imaginary life and world of young children is very rich and very real for them and this continues to be the case until their more logical and rational left brain has fully matured. So the window for magical thinking and imagination is quite small and we should nurture it in our children while we can and for as long as we can because it underpins important brain and behavioural development in them ... and also because it's nice to believe in magic at an age when we can do so unquestioningly!

15-minute Practice: Magical thinking

Here are some practical ways in which you can invest in your child's magical and imaginative thinking experiences.

Reading is a wonderful way to introduce your child to a world of magical thinking or to further stimulate your child's imagination. Choose books that are not related to a TV show but that celebrate the power of children. Start with the books that gave you pleasure when you were a child; your children will love to hear what stories you read when you were their age.

Gather up the miniatures and mini towns, houses, trees, fences and animals and encourage your children to create **small worlds.** They will play happily at this themselves and will also welcome you into their world should you be able to meet them there. If you do join them in this type of play, remember it is their play and you should follow their lead. If your child needs some support with this type of play you can start the story and bring them into it or ask them to finish the story you started. Involve them in setting the scene and wonder what else you will need to complete the scene to get them more actively involved.

Shared storytelling is where everyone takes a turn in making up a story. You can do this from your heads or use a prop to guide you. If you are making it up, one of you starts with one line. (I like to start with *Once upon a time* as that line immediately makes it possible for anything to happen in the story. It's the start of most magical stories and hearing it tells your children that the story does not have to be 'real' and this further stimulates their imagination.) The next person adds another line and so on. You follow the twists and turns that get added to the story without questioning or trying to guide it in a certain way.

Roleplay is a great way to enter your child's magical world of imagination with them. Put on your dress-up clothes and follow their lead as you both *become* make-believe characters and play out a story together.

You can give your child some empty jam jars or other containers and allow them to mix water with things like flower petals, a few drops of food colouring, essential oil or a sprinkle of glitter. They can mix it into jars of **potions** or **perfume**.

Take your child's favourite book, movie or TV show and allow them to **make up their own ending**. Tell them to imagine they are the author/director and they get to say 'Cut!' and change something about the story. Have them draw what they would add or change and tell you how this would change the story and what the new ending would be. They can draw this but they could also use the small world miniatures and play it out for you.

....

CHAPTER 9

The Politics of Play

Play dates are a modern parenting phenomenon. I managed to get through my entire childhood without my parents organising a play date for me and I am fine. But they are a part of today's parenting and childhood. If you are parenting a single child you may find them a positive way of ensuring your child has time with other children outside school. But in any case, children do not *need* play dates; they may want them and even enjoy them, but they do not developmentally need them. They are a parental choice rather than a necessity.

Some parents manage play dates without any stress. For others they are all about walking a fine line of not offending anyone and remembering to reciprocate. I have also worked with parents who openly admit to using structured play dates as a means of managing their children's friendships, admitting that they target certain playmates for their children who they believe will be a good influence. I do not believe it is about whether or not it is right for parents to 'target' playmates for their children in an upwardly mobile way, simply because children will negotiate friendships for themselves (usually) without any parental input and if they do not feel a connection with the children you select for them to play with, it won't last.

Another word on play dates. They should not be confused with babysitting and they work best when there is some structure to them. I appreciate the temptation to send your children on a play date to free up your afternoon to get chores or some self-care done in peace, and perhaps you can enjoy a reciprocal arrangement with like-minded parents, but please be aware that this is what you are doing and that this type of lengthy play date on adult terms may not suit the children. Play dates work best when there are no more than three or four children involved at any one time (including the hosting child). Many children prefer one-on-one play dates; if that's the case, respect that preference and do not overwhelm them. Ninety minutes is plenty of time for a play date after school, 60 minutes for very young children. You want the play date to end on a positive note where the children want more of each other rather than waiting for an inevitable row to emerge as they get tired and want/need alone time to process their day. Many children will manage their play date well themselves, they will be able to play independently of you and find activities that interest and include their friend. Other children may need some structure, especially if they find sharing and turn-taking hard or struggle to allow the other child to choose an activity as well. You might consider structuring the beginning and end of this play date and err on the side of a shorter duration until they can manage them better themselves. You can achieve this by, for example, having a baking activity (e.g. cookies or fairy cakes) ready to go at the start, and then they can go and play independently while the item is baking and return to decorate it towards the end.

CHOOSING FRIENDS

It is rare enough that children require input from their parents around their friendships or play date activities. In general, children play naturally and without interference from parents. There is developmental importance in how children make friends as well, and parents should not interfere with this. At pre-school age children will be friends with everyone in their group in crèche/Montessori; once they start primary school they begin to try out and explore a variety of friendship dynamics because they are exploring themselves and the world around them. They will often be 'best friends' with a child for a period of time and then not want to play with that same child ever again. And from the age of approximately seven years they will have settled on who they want to be friends with, and while they may have some falling-outs they will generally be their friends for school. Interfering with this process to suit your own parental agenda (trying to have your children be friends with the children of your own friends) or social agenda (wanting to secure your children a particular social setting through their friends) denies them access to the natural developmental process.

Let your child take the lead and pick their own friends. It can be tempting to try to orchestrate it so that your children are friends with the children of your own friends, but if this doesn't work out you may put your own friendship at risk; and we adults need our friendships as we grow older, just as much as our children do, so take care of the ones you have – they're yours and you matter. Children know who they want to play with and who they like being around, so ask your child who they would like to invite over to play. It is developmentally good for them to experience what it's like to find and develop friendships with like-minded children, which makes it easier to connect with and communicate naturally with peers as they get older and even into adulthood. This also helps them to develop instincts as to who is a good or perhaps inappropriate friend for themselves. Children should not be profiled and pigeon-holed according to their background, and achievement and ambition should never be reduced merely to academic prowess. People are not made this way and it is important that children learn early on that people are all different and everyone has different but equally important qualities that should be appreciated and valued.

The older children get, the deeper and more complex their reflections and perspectives on their friends and friendships become. Initially friendships are momentary and transient and really *all about them*. As they grow and start primary school their friendships take on a more *self-serving* tone as children seek out playmates who make them feel good about themselves, complement their temperament and do nice things for them. Later (over seven years old and up to pre-adolescence), their friendships are *more reciprocal* and they can better consider the needs, feelings and perspectives of their friends, and these considerations will affect how they feel about and select their friendships. This is why it is around this time that children tend to settle into their friendship clusters that will take them through junior school and some that will continue beyond that phase. In pre-adolescence and adolescence friendships become *more intimate and respectful*, and children/young people genuinely care about each other's emotional wellbeing. This phase allows them to gradually become less possessive of their friends and to tolerate and stick by each other in good times and bad.

These guidelines are exactly that, guidelines; they are not rules for every child. You will know a lot more about the type of friend your child is and the type of friend your child wants/needs by simply observing them. Young babies show excitement and joy at seeing other young babies from about six months old. They often think that other babies are toys and they grab and pull at them as though they were a teddy or doll. They will flail their arms and make high-pitched noises as a means of engaging the other child. By toddlerhood (12–18 months) they show a capacity to actively play with other children of the same age and may even start to show some preference for particular children whom they see more often. Older toddlers (up to three years of age) can show empathy and kindness towards each other. You will observe this in how they will pat the arm of an upset peer or try to kiss a scraped knee better for their friend or gently take their hands. And while these kind and gentle behaviours may be infrequent amidst the general rough and tumble, it does show that they are not entirely self-absorbed at this age.

So this is how children come together as friends and it is important you interfere as little as possible as they negotiate these various developments in their friendships. But what do you do if your child should fall out with their friends or find himself or herself the victim of bullying? My message here is largely the same – you should stay out of the ups and downs of childhood friendships as much as you can *unless* they cross the line into bullying. Then you must step in.

BULLYING

We need to be very clear about what is and is not bullying, as it is a word that has become somewhat casualised around children. Bullying is conscious, strategic and focused negative attention targeting a child verbally, physically or through isolation and is a repeated pattern of behaviour. It may be one child bullying another or it can be one child who encourages others to join in targeting one other child. It is a problem and must be addressed with parents and the school or wherever it is happening as promptly as possible. All children have a right to feel safe in school, at home and as they go about their various activities. That being said, there is a difference between *bullying* and *rudeness/meanness*. A child not wanting to play with another child might be rude and unpleasant but in and of itself this does not constitute bullying. A child saying something nasty to another or isolating a child from the game on a single occasion might be mean, but a once-off occasion does not constitute bullying. We are not going to be doing our children any favours if we label every spat they experience with other children as bullying; neither are we helping them if we rush into the school (or wherever) every time they come home a little upset about something that happened between them and another child.

I have spoken with a lot of children about negative experiences they have had in school and I find that they are not always seeking someone to jump in and fix the issues for them. Rather, they want to have someone listen as they think it all through out loud. So let's take this approach and imagine your child tells you about something mean or rude another child did to them at school that day. Your child is downcast about the experience and you can tell that they are upset by it. Your parental hackles are up and you have a burning desire to rush down to the school and have the teacher intervene or tell the other child off for this behavioural transgression towards your child. Of course you feel like this; you are a loving parent who wants only the best for your child. But is this type of intervention the best thing for your child? Maybe, maybe not.

Here is how you will learn to tell the difference. After your child has told you what has happened, seek to know more by being curious and empathic but not challenging. 'I can see that you feel sad about this. I'm sorry something happened to make you feel this way. I wasn't there, so can you help me understand what happened a bit more? Tell me the story again but start from just before the bad thing happened and tell it right up to what happened afterwards too.' Sit facing your child at their eye level, holding their hands in yours, and attentively listen as they tell you the story. You might have a few questions or clarifications, but try to limit these interruptions and just listen. Then repeat back a brief summary of what you have heard. 'So you really wanted to play that same game from yesterday during break time but today X wouldn't let you play with them and that made you feel sad. Even though you felt sad, you found someone else to play with. Is that right?' Allow your child a final chance to correct you in case you have misunderstood. When you feel you have it clear and have reflected back what they have told you with empathy, you could say, 'I wonder if there is something you want me to do about this situation or can you handle it yourself?' If your child says they can handle it, let them handle it. This doesn't mean you don't check in with them a few days later to ask how that situation worked out, but don't be surprised if they've now forgotten all about it and moved on.

We want to encourage critical and solution-focused thinking in our children, along with strong emotional resilience. This will not happen if we fix everything for them, and many children tell me that they just want someone to listen to them and do not want their parents to go in and sort it out for them.

If you have a child who will defer to you to fix everything you might want to encourage them to **attempt a solution themselves** first. You might say, 'I now understand what happened and how you feel about it. I wonder what you think you could do to make this better?' Listen as they suggest some solutions. You might give them a nudge towards one over the other, or better again, roleplay it with your story stem doll set (Chapter 7) so that your child can see what it will look and sound like in action. It can also help to have them consider all perspectives. For example, 'I wonder how the other child might have been feeling?', 'I wonder what you would suggest if this happened to your friend and you wanted to help them feel better or fix it?', etc.

Perhaps you have a child who is clearly bothered and distressed but will not tell you about what has happened and certainly would not want you to go in to do anything about it on their behalf. You will need to wonder and wonder and wonder. 'I see something is bothering you and that makes me wonder if something happened during your day that maybe it would help to talk about.' If this is a no-go, invite them to draw a picture that shows what happened. Use the **movie/director technique** here and tell them to pretend that what happened is a scene from a movie and they are the director so they can yell 'Cut!' like directors do when they are making a movie. Now they get to edit the scene, i.e., draw another picture about how they wish this scene had gone, including what all the characters would have to have done to help it go better. Invite them to talk about this during or afterwards, but they do not have to if they choose not to. Trust that something will have shifted and processed for them in the activity. It can be tempting to demand that we know everything that is going on but some children, especially self-holding children (more about this in Chapter 13), will not want to share their experiences in this way and really, your aim is that they process the experience and feel better about it.

With all these approaches I have suggested that you check back with your child a few days later to ensure that the situation has been managed. If it has not been resolved or has escalated, you will need to ask, 'I wonder if there is something I could help with now,' and see how your child is feeling about it. If it has escalated to a level that you are uneasy with, say something like, 'I think you did a great job trying to work this out, but now I feel this is something I should talk to your teacher/scout leader/football coach about.'

If you have a mild concern – you think your child is experiencing something negative that is affecting them but you do not have concrete information, just a hunch and observing their emotional patterns – you should arrange to talk to their teacher (or activity leader). Voice your concerns and ask if they could support your child by keeping a closer eye on what might be happening. Perhaps the teacher/coach has already observed something themselves or can offer you some reassurance that all is okay.

Essentially this is all about balance. You want to instil a sense of empowerment in your child so that they are emotionally resilient enough to withstand day-to-day spats with their peers, have a level of confidence and skill to negotiate through disagreements and engage in repair where necessary and know that there are always other perspectives on every situation, which will equip them with empathy and strong critical thinking skills. However, you also want them to bring this stuff to you, the small stuff and the big stuff, and to trust that you will be interested and curious and will listen empathically while allowing them to work out a solution. But if the situation is too big or too serious they will know they can ask you to step in for them.

In order for this to work, both at this young age (up to seven years) and later, when they are teenagers, they have to see you as the parent-in-charge. You are not their friend and you are not trying to be friends with their friends (this is especially important as they get older). This means that you have to be comfortable not always being seen as cool and taking the tough stance when necessary. You are saying clearly that you will follow their lead where possible but will step in and take charge when necessary. And while they may not overtly thank you for this right now they will appreciate your stance as they grow up. Holding this consistent and predictable parental line is also very reassuring to your children and gives them a sense of safety.

When we instil in our children a strong sense of self, confidence and self-belief, healthy capacity for critical and solution-focused thinking, empathy and perspective-taking, courage in making repair when they have experienced a falling-out with peers, we are raising them to be emotionally resilient. Emotionally resilient people not only believe in themselves but also in the good in others and the world around them. They accept that sometimes bad things happen but believe they will work through those times. They know that you do not always have to have the answers and that neither does anyone else (parents included), but you can seek to work out answers by sharing your thoughts and feelings with others. They can be happy when they have nothing to do because boredom doesn't overwhelm them. They have a good sense of boundaries and limits and they know when something is getting too big, too much or too out of control. They adapt well to new situations and new rules and expectations.

If this describes your child, fantastic – well done. If it does not describe your child, don't panic – it is never too late to start building resilience. Indeed, it is a journey that starts in childhood, but we continue to nurture and develop emotional resilience throughout our lives. Start with some of the strategies about your children's play dates and friendships and school life listed above. Make and hold clear, logical, consistent and predictable boundaries so that your child knows what is expected of them.

Invest in an emotional language. Help your child understand that they are made up of lots of feeling parts. *Parts language* is very helpful when building emotional resilience in children. It lets them know that they are not the angry/anxious/sad child in your family, because one emotion does not define who they are – it is merely a *part* of who they are. This teaches them that they can find ways to access other feeling parts of themselves and identify these parts in others. You can achieve this by talking about how you can see their sad or angry part because X has happened. Empathise and show you understand the justification for their feeling. Then 'wonder' with them what you might do together to bring out their happy or calm part. And then do that with them.

Leading by example is always the most effective parenting strategy because our children take their emotional and behavioural lead from us parents. So you can model solution-focused thinking in your life and share with them (appropriate) examples of how this has worked well for you. Ensure that you keep the lines of communication between you and your child open so that they know they can come to you, no matter how good or bad the situation is, and that even if you're not pleased with them you will support them and help them through whatever it is. Help them to know that communication is not just about words and talking about things but that there are other ways to connect and process something, hence using art/balloons/ play activities to help them express their emotions from a very young age.

Talk about and share your family stories so that they internalise that they are a part of a bigger system and that everyone has good and bad experiences but can come through almost anything together. Stimulate creativity and imagination in this way as well by making up stories together as a family or creating a 'Who Done It?' scenario whereby you create a mystery crime (something age-appropriate like 'who stole the cookie' or 'the mystery of the missing sock') and tell a story that contains some hints for them to pick up. You could also leave more clues for them to discover around the house until they come up with the answer by working it out together. Get involved yourself and then get your children involved in your community; this gives a strong sense of belonging and of how important it is to work together and invest in our environment outside our immediate family. Reach out and communicate with your school, your children's activity leaders and your childcare providers (as applicable) and let them know that you have concerns about your child or if you are taking a new approach to help them build their emotional resilience and how they might be able to help you with this.

Empathy is one of the most crucial life skills we can teach our young children and it is one of those things that we start when they're young and keep going as they grow up. You can't sit your child down and give them a lecture or lesson on *what is empathy* because we want them to *feel* it, not just *think* it. It is something we can talk about to some degree, but mostly it is something we model by doing. It takes many years to fully grasp an understanding of empathy, but this doesn't mean we should wait until our children are older to begin teaching it.

When it comes to teaching empathy, remember:

E – Everybody needs somebody (encouragement and support of others is valuable).

M – Model and Mirror (if you model then they will mirror you, so lead by example).

P – Perspective-taking. Put yourself in their shoes (use 'wondering' – ask your child, 'I wonder how you would feel if this happened to you and what would make you feel better' – and use this to put yourself in your child's shoes too).

A – Ask if you can help (we want to encourage autonomy where possible and be available to help when necessary).

T – Treat others as you would like to be treated yourself (ask, 'How would this make you feel? And what would you like someone to do if this was happening to you?').

H – Hurtful or Helpful (use your parenting pause button to encourage your child to stop and ask themselves if something they are doing/saying is hurtful or helpful to the other person).

Y – You feel better, they feel better (being kind is good for everyone).

15-minute practice: Building empathy

When something is fun it becomes appealing and that gives young children a positive association with it. Here are some ways that you can build empathy-teaching moments into your parenting.

Collect some large stones when you are out for a walk. Wash them when at home and once they are dried you can engage your child in painting them. Once dry they can be gifted as **paper weights** to neighbours/family members.

Plant a seed with your child. Each day they must take care of and nurture their seed as it grows into a flower or plant. This gives them something to do each day and you can praise their kindness and thoughtfulness.

Let your child see you randomly **leave some money** on a parking machine or a vending machine so that somebody can benefit.

Let your child see you **pay for an extra beverage** when you are in the café and say that it is for the next person or for somebody who might need it that day.

Have your child help you pack **care packages** and then go with them to drop them off at a homeless shelter or soup kitchen.

Encourage your child to **re-gift toys** to children in shelters/ orphanages or to buy a new toy for a child who is less well off.

Let your child see you **hold doors open** for people coming behind you.

When with your child, stop to ask someone with heavy bags or full hands if they would like some **help**.

Involve your child in **making breakfast** in bed for a family member.

Always say **please** and **thank you** to your child - even if this is 'Please don't hit my foot with your truck.'

Remember to smile when you see your child so that they know you are happy to see them, no matter what else has been going on in the day.

....

CHAPTER 10

Help! My Child Wants More Independence ... Or None at All

We all experience the conflict between wanting our children to be more independent and being terrified at the first sign of independence. So how do we strike a balance between giving our children the opportunity to assert themselves and grow as, and into, independent beings while maintaining parental control at the same time?

An essential part of growing up is testing and pushing parental boundaries and (gradually) gaining more and more independence so that we can become independent and self-sufficient adults. This is increasingly becoming an era of parents micro-managing their children's lives, and parents (and children) have now become accustomed to adults meeting all their children's needs for them. We need to find a balance between allowing children to do things for themselves and providing the necessary support and guidance to ensure that they make good and safe choices.

As your child begins to demand more independence and to pull away from you a little, this is the perfect time to teach them responsibility because independence and responsibility go hand in hand. The more responsible your children can show you they have become, the easier it is for you to relax and support their independence. Children begin to demand independence from a very young age; there is no one more wilful in this regard than a two-year-old child asserting, 'I do myself.' And how wonderful it is to see them do this. It is your child's job to pull against you and demand this freedom and your job as a parent to drip feed them their independence in a staged, age-appropriate and developmentally appropriate way, ensuring that you are preparing them adequately along the way.

If you can make choices, decision-making and gradual independence a part of your child's upbringing they will be better prepared to manage and keep themselves safe when they are independent. This is a normal part of your child's journey to adulthood. Children must get to try out new things and take risks ... with your guidance and support. You are the expert on your child and nobody knows your child better than you, so trust your instincts and if you believe that your child is ready to walk to the shop or to a friend's house on their own, you can allow this. Give them a time to be back by or an instruction to call when they have arrived safely to reassure you if this helps.

Essentially, independence is a process that starts in young childhood and continues into young adulthood and beyond. Create as many safe and controlled opportunities for your child to develop their sense of independence as you can from a young age and gradually increase these as they get older and more responsible. It can be hard as a parent to accept that your child is growing up and pulling away from you. Reflect on how much of your reluctance to give more independence is down to your child and how much is down to your own anxiety.

As parents we can make the mistake of doing things for our children that we know they can do for themselves. Sometimes this is because children are so very good at delay tactics that by the fifth time you've asked them to get dressed for school but they are still sitting at the kitchen table in their pyjamas or wandering around upstairs saying they can't find things, you will flip and end up undressing and dressing them if only to get you all out of the door on time. This is totally understandable, relatable and everyone has been there. But if this becomes a habit, if you are routinely doing things for your child that you know they can quite competently manage for themselves, you risk sending the message that you do not have faith in your child's ability to do things for themselves. This can result in a situation of *learned helplessness* whereby your child won't even try to do things for themselves, which will have a knock-on effect on their self-esteem and general social skills. Instead use things like the sand timer or the colour-coded clock. As a last resort, remind them that they are old enough to dress themselves but if they are late because they choose not to do so they must tell the teacher themselves why they are late.

Remember, your child should want to be independent and you will find this a challenge at times, but you should both try to be open to taking (controlled) risks by allowing them to try things from a young age. It is good for young children's development to be encouraged to face challenges and engage in risk-taking activities throughout their childhood. As teenagers, their brains are neurologically wired to take risks, so as much as possible we want to direct them towards positive over negative risk-taking and this needs to start way before adolescence. Fear conditioning begins early and it has a gendered lens. Research shows that parents are four times more likely to urge their daughters to be careful about trying something physical while encouraging their sons to do precisely that[7]. This may make our girls less likely than our boys to try challenging physical activities, which are crucial in developing new skills and can lead to a more sedentary and passive lifestyle for girls. The fact is that challenge and risk-taking activities are directly linked to our children's self-esteem. We need to expose our young children to stories and opportunities where courage, exploration and exciting deeds are available to them. If we expose them to appropriate levels of positive risk-taking behaviour it is almost certain that they will struggle a little and even fail at times. Remember, though, that misadventure means they will learn to try again and that mishap is a fundamental part of early childhood and the pursuit of independence.

If your child refuses to try to do things that you know are well within their developmental grasp but they are showing signs of *learned helplessness* it may be a cause for concern, but it can absolutely be dealt with by you at home. First you need to work out why they are reluctant to try out new things. Is it because of fear of failure or because they haven't had much opportunity to do things for themselves? Sit down with them and, using positive language, tell them that you are so proud of them and how they are growing up every day. Add that part of growing up is that you get to do some things all for yourself. Say that you are always so proud and happy when you see them trying to do things themselves rather than waiting for you to do them. Suggest you make a list of three to five everyday things that you know they can do for themselves and from now on they will do these things without your help. You can review and increase this list bit by bit and ideally you want to get to a place where your child is identifying what they can do for themselves without your input.

There are many practical ways of giving your child opportunities to practise independence. Encourage your child to do the things they can do for themselves. For example, smaller children need a lot of assistance from adults to reach things and get things, so when there's something your child can get for themselves, perhaps a cup from the counter, the cheese from the fridge or a book from a low shelf, encourage them to do so, and praise their efforts.

It is always advisable to encourage your children to **problem solve** from a very young age as this facilitates confidence and independent thinking. When your child is struggling with something and asks you to do it or fix it or answer it for them, stop and encourage them to think of a way they can work it out themselves. Depending on their age, you could suggest they write a pros and cons list or draw a picture of the choices they have and see which one they think is best for them.

Children should be encouraged to make decisions from a young age from which outfit or shoes to wear, to whether they want chicken or fish for dinner, to choosing which storybook they want before bed.

CHORES

Chores are good for children. They give them a sense of responsibility and independence and a feeling that they are part of a family system bigger than themselves. They learn that part of being in a family is that everyone helps out, and children like being able to help. There should always be some chores that children must do without being paid for them. If you want to tie their pocket money to chores, assign additional tasks that you can pay them for doing. When it comes to what age to start assigning chores, the truth is that you can start from as young as two years old.

Two to three years old

- Carry their own nappies to the bin and throw them out
- Pick up their own toys and put them into a toy box

Four to five years old

- Put away their toys
- Help tidy their bedroom

- Wipe down the outside of the bin with a damp cloth
- Put cutlery into the cutlery drawer
- Carry laundry to the laundry basket
- Put their pyjamas under their pillow after they are dressed

Six to seven years old

All of the above and ...

- Fold towels
- Carry clean laundry to their bedroom and put it away neatly
- Straighten the duvet on their bed after they get up
- Unload the dishwasher (leaving things they cannot reach on the counter top for you to do)

Eight to nine years old

All of the above and ...

- Set the table and clear the table after meals
- Wash dishes
- Take the bin out on bin collection day and bring it back in when it is empty
- Take care of family pets (feed them, etc.)
- Make their bed and tidy their bedroom
- Light dusting

Just because they *can* do all of these doesn't mean you assign *all* of these chores. Pick two to three chores that are developmentally appropriate for your child and stick with those, occasionally changing the chores you assign them.

This list is not exhaustive. Add to it yourself with what tasks you know your child can do. Once you have identified such opportunities you may wish to focus in on some priorities rather than giving your child 20 responsibilities all at once. Build in additional time to your daily routine to ensure they get to do their tasks.

Praise effort over outcome – do not freak out if the milk gets spilled on its way to the cereal bowl, because milk cartons are heavy to hold until you are used to them. Instead say, 'Sometimes things spill. Let me show you how to clean that up so you can do it next time.'

If your child is unwell or overwhelmed with something else that is going on, modify your expectations accordingly and give them a pass.

POCKET MONEY

Pocket money is another good and practical way to introduce independence and responsibility, so it can be useful to plan ahead and start a system young that you can adapt it as your child grows, gradually increasing their sense of autonomy and independence in line with their evolving development. I think pocket money is a great idea and I also believe that you can start giving pocket money at a very young age, certainly from four years onwards. I believe it is good to teach children about money and its value from a young age along with the importance of saving for larger desired items. It helps them to appreciate that you work for the money to buy them what they need and that things have to be earned and saved for. Beyond this, having their own money enables them to make choices, consider options and go into a shop to buy something and interact with sales staff independently. These are important life skills that also help develop a sense of empowerment and confidence that will spill into other areas of your child's life.

The many child development benefits to giving your child pocket money include:

- It encourages independence.
- It helps develop budgeting skills and an appreciation of the value of money.
- By affording them the opportunity to decide on things they like and want, they are developing a capacity for desire.
- It can help them develop saving skills – to this end it is a good idea to start a practice that they automatically save 10% of whatever amount you give them.

The amount you give is absolutely up to you and should be influenced by your family's financial situation but also by your child's age and stage of development.

You can decide if pocket money should be earned by doing household tasks, but I would add here that part of being in a family is the expectation that everyone helps out, so I would suggest that there are set chores/tasks that your child is responsible for that they are *not* paid for, but you could offer them the opportunity to take on additional chores to earn money. If you do this, be consistent with it and if the chore/task is not done properly they do not get paid for it.

What do you expect their pocket money to cover? Are they to buy their own phone credit or personal items (teenagers) or do you cover these and their pocket money is for extra or treat items? The amount you give should reflect this and you should be clear with your child from the outset; perhaps have a pocket money agreement you both sign up to. Do not be swayed by what you are told their friends get. You are responsible for parenting your child so you must develop your own system and stick to it.

If you want pocket money to be an effective developmental tool, stick to your own budget as much as you want them to learn to stick to theirs. What I mean is that when it's gone, it's gone – you do not top it up during the week. This way your child learns moderation and how to make their money stretch to last the whole week. If there is a busy week coming up in a month (perhaps someone's birthday or an outing with friends) when you know they will need more money, encourage them to save a percentage of their weekly money so that they have extra for a more expensive week.

....

15-minute practice: Supermarkets

Sometimes affording your children independence is for their benefit; at other times it can be a great help to you too. For example, supermarkets are tricky places for children because in addition to being bright, big and noisy with temperature changes depending on which aisle you are in, they're not allowed to touch everything, they might not like being in the trolley, they want to leave, they distract you while you're looking for items. As a result, supermarkets are the scene of many a child meltdown and flustered parent trying to manage said meltdown while battling a packed trolley. As you know only too well, it is very hard to co-regulate a hyper-aroused child when we are feeling flustered and under pressure ourselves. It can feel as though everyone is looking at you thinking, 'Wouldn't you think that parent would put manners on that child?', though in reality most people looking at you are just relieved it's not happening to them.

I developed my **supermarket saviour system** because children do better when they feel that something is happening *with them* rather than *to them*. This is why it's a good idea to involve them in the exercise and give them an active role in the grocery shopping process. Then they will be occupied, stimulated and engaged in the process and this is a sure way to defend against tantrums.

- You will need to do one site visit to your local supermarket to familiarise yourself with what is on each aisle and select a couple of items that are at your child's level, i.e. top shelf if the child is in the trolley, bottom shelf if they are walking around. Plan to skip the treats aisle when your child is with you to avoid unnecessary tensions.
- You will also need a sheet of coloured paper, some markers and pictures of appropriate, accessible food items.

- Make a special shopping list for your child to be in charge of when they come with you. Assign them responsibility for one or two items per aisle from their own list, ticking off each item as they get them.

- It can be nice to include a counting item such as 'four tomatoes', so that you can offer additional praise for their great counting skills.

- They might also have their own shopping bag to carry their items out of the shop and unpack when you get home.

Shopping List

	Milk	☐
	6 Eggs	☐
	Butter	☐
	Bread	☐
	3 Apples	☐
	4 Bananas	☐

CHOICES

Another great way to give children experience of independence is via choices. However, a child should never be in a position of making a choice that affects the whole family. In other words, nothing so big that it impacts on everyone else. So avoid open-ended options such as 'Where do you want to go?' and replace them with 'Would you like to go to the park or the woods?' Instead of 'What would you like to drink?' – which may elicit a request for a fizzy drink or something that was never an option, which you now have to battle about – say, 'Would you like milk or water with your dinner?' Only give choice options that you are entirely happy with and your child gets to express and explore independence and preference within your boundaries.

In summary, independence is very good for your child, but it doesn't just happen. You must take small, steady and developmentally appropriate steps from early on to nurture their drive for independence and then gradually increase their opportunities to experience it more and more as they grow.

15-minute practice: Transitions

Change and transitions can be very difficult for children and there is a fine line between preparing them for upcoming change and overburdening them with the details of it. You might find that your child regresses a little in terms of independence and might even become clingier and want you to do things you know they can do themselves. Learning how to manage and negotiate through change and transitions is another independence milestone for your child.

A simple yet effective way to help them negotiate transitions is to use a visual **storyboard** that outlines the change in eight simple steps.

This technique can be used to introduce change in a daily routine; a house move; potty training; how to behave in a restaurant; how to travel safely in the car; or any situation where you expect your child to behave in a particular way. You will need:

- A large sheet of coloured poster card
- Markers
- Pictures/photos/drawings. The method you use is up to you. Some children like to pose for photos, which further personalises the storyboard, or you can use pictures sourced online or draw them yourself if you prefer.

In eight steps (because this is enough for them to have to hold in mind), show your child what you expect of them in a situation. A sample board might go:

1. Getting up
2. Eating breakfast
3. Brushing teeth and getting dressed
4. How you travel to school/childcare
5. Being in school/childcare
6. Coming home
7. Having a snack with you/doing homework
8. Going to bed.

This works because if your child becomes dysregulated and wants to go home, telling them that they will see mum/dad at two o'clock is too abstract, but if they can picture the board in their minds and know they are just two pictures away from getting back to you they can better manage their feelings in the moment.

....

CHAPTER 11

Discipline

This is probably one of the topics I am most often asked about. It is also one about which other people feel compelled to tell you what you should be doing and one the older generation will shake their heads over as they lament, 'In my day children were seen and not heard/knew how to behave/respected their elders/a slap never did me any harm', etc.

To be successful with discipline you have to start by reflecting on what discipline means to you. Ask yourself how you were disciplined as a child and how you felt about that. How you choose to discipline your child is exactly that, your choice. What follows here is intended to support you in shaping your own discipline system that you feel confident about and that you know will work with your child.

I am often asked what discipline is, what its purpose is and what the best methods are. My answer is always the same. Discipline is about teaching, not punishing and not coercing, and it must be consistent and creative yet logical. When I say that discipline is not about punishment, it may be appropriate that punishment be a part of discipline – in which case it should quickly/immediately follow the misbehaviour, be brief and be respectful of your child's feelings and stage of development. It's also very important to reconnect with your child in a positive way soon afterwards. However, the main purpose of discipline should always be to teach your child a lesson and not just to punish misbehaviour!

So what message do you want to teach? If you take this approach you should ask yourself, 'What am I teaching my child in this discipline?' Is it time-out, grounding or losing privileges or something else? Be clear about the message you are teaching and ensure your discipline measure fits your chosen agenda. Assess your child's ability to self-discipline before deciding on the discipline measure. For example, a child under two years will show a lack of boundaries (having not yet fully negotiated the second attachment cycle where boundaries and limits are taught and internalised) and will require consistent and repeated reminding of what is appropriate and what is not – consistency is vital here.

A child under four years old cannot (consistently) understand cause and effect, so disciplining them can prove a futile endeavour that frustrates you without effecting meaningful change in your child's behaviour. For children under four I suggest you employ strategies of distraction/redirection over discipline. This is not to say that you ignore what has happened. Take their hands in yours and either gently sway them or rub small circles on the back of their hands with yours as you slowly come down to their eye level. Hold their hands because coming down to the eye level of an angry toddler is unwise unless you want a punch in the face. You use gentle rhythm and touch because these trigger the sub-systems of the brain associated with emotional regulation. Once at their eye level you say in a clear, firm yet gentle voice, 'No. We do not do X. Now show me your game/toy/painting/Play-Doh,' and redirect them, staying engaged with them until you know that the moment has passed and they have successfully co-regulated their emotional state with yours and are now sufficiently calm to return to their previous activity or other children they were playing with.

Sometimes an older child will also display a lack of boundaries and act out, so you must decide whether your child knows that there is a boundary, has crossed it on purpose and is testing your limits. Perhaps your child cheekily smiles while they break the rules/boundary; the message here is that they need you to step in and hold the boundary without getting angry with them. This may look like defiant behaviour, but it is not; your child is displaying a need and a sense of inner turmoil in that they know they are breaking a rule and want you to see them do it. Try to proactively deal with this one by stopping and saying, 'It makes me so happy when you show me and everyone else what a great friend you are when you play nicely with other children,' and give them a high five; do this before you take them to a birthday party, for example, where you know they will have a tendency to get over-stimulated and act out.

So-called 'acting-out behaviours' are often dismissed as 'attention-seeking', but what if this apparent need for attention is actually a need for connection? I believe that a child's overt behaviour is actually a communication of an emotional state that is driven by a need for human emotional connection. Remember, we all just want the people closest to us to *get us* so that we can *feel felt* or *get gotten* by the ones we love. From infancy, through the transitions from childhood into adolescence and then to young adulthood, children need emotional connection with their parent. The parent–child relationship forms a secure base from where they can go out and explore the world and have independent experiences, and equally important, that is a safe haven that they can return to when things get too challenging and overwhelming.

BOUNDARIES AND COMMUNICATION

Threats, rules and rewards might initially succeed in controlling your child's behaviour, but the mechanisms of stickers, treats and time-outs become less effective over time. What will achieve long-lasting and meaningful change are your unconditional love and your *presence* over your *presents*. Children behave well when they feel secure in their emotional connectedness and safe in their parents' love. Love does not mean giving in or acquiescing to their demands; quite the opposite – our children, regardless of their age or stage of development, need us parents to be available, reliable, gentle yet firm. This means setting and holding boundaries and limits while taking the time to stop and reflect and seek to understand your child's inner emotional world so that you can help them to make sense of the confusion growing up causes.

Boundaries and clear, calm, consistent limit-setting are vital to nurture your child's development. This helps to create predictable, reliable and safe environments, which ultimately lead to a stronger sense of security and safety for children. Limits and boundaries let your child know that you will make sure that they don't go too far or that the situation won't get beyond their control because you will use your limit-setting to make it safe.

Clear communication is an absolute must if you want to have a bonding relationship with your child. It helps to build a foundation of trust, fosters a healthy level of self-esteem, encourages positive behaviour and helps tone down frustration and stress in the whole family. So talk often with your child to bring out positive opinions, ideas and behaviours by using an affirmative tone and body language. Treat your child with the same respect with which you would have them treat you. Say 'Hi', 'I love you', 'How was your day?', even, and perhaps especially, if they are pushing you away. Do things together both one-on-one and with the whole family (as detailed in Chapter 6). Never shut your child out to show that you disapprove of their behaviour. If you need time before you can talk to them about something that has upset you, tell them that you need time. Don't walk away and be silent. You are the parent, and because of this, you do have the final say. Children know this and trust you because of it. But do try to explain your reasoning whenever possible. And enjoy each other, because when you teach your child that they can enjoy relating and be enjoyed by others you are empowering them to develop and sustain healthy relationships in their life beyond you.

Above all else, be consistent. Communicating clear and consistent boundaries takes away uncertainty for your child. Focus on teaching as opposed to punishing and your child will begin to develop an internal system of self-discipline, which allows them to develop the capacity to shape and manage their own behaviour, including making good and positive decisions.

DISCIPLINE STRATEGIES

My overarching message on this topic is that discipline should teach the behaviour you want to see rather than punish the behaviour you don't want to see. Your discipline strategies must fit with your child and their developmental stage. This means you will need different discipline strategies for different children in your family, but generally this means tweaking your overall strategy rather than having an entirely different strategy for each child. Your beliefs and principles remain the same.

Ideally, any discipline strategies you use should be quick, creative, effective and help to return you and your child to a calmer and more connected place. Creative discipline is especially effective with children of any age.

We all know that if you enter into a battle of wills with a small child, you will lose. Learn to pick your battles and save serious discipline for serious transgressions – don't sweat the small stuff. If your child starts to throw a temper tantrum because they cannot have sweets before dinner, rather than start battling with them over it, your best option is to try to distract your child by giving them a job to do, such as, 'Can you try to find the baked beans in the back of the press and bring me a tin, please?'

I also recommend the 'choices and consequences model'. We all know the 'You're not the boss of me' stand-off, so here's a suggestion. Try saying, 'You're right, I'm not the boss of what you choose to do, but I am the boss of what happens when you do it! You can choose to behave nicely, as I know you can, and I decide that you get a high five for that; or you can choose to break the rules and behave badly and I will decide that you cannot use your computer game this afternoon. But you're in charge of what you do, so it's up to you!' This teaches them that they have control over their own behaviour but that you will make sure that the boundary is consistent, which is reassuring in itself.

Children who are emotionally injured, such as adopted and/or fostered children and children living in residential care environments, need different considerations when being disciplined. Children from emotionally disrupted backgrounds are often coming into your family from a place that may have had dramatically different standards of acceptable behaviours as well as a different standard as to what constituted discipline. Children with this type of background may also have a delay in their ability to control impulse behaviours and a low frustration tolerance and these must be factored into any discipline measures. Such children can find it very difficult to hold in mind that you can be angry with their behaviour but still love and care for them. I would suggest using discipline with children like this with great caution, because this child's chronological age may be very different to their developmental age. Be creative with your discipline strategies and always build in the opportunity for making repair. The consequence for their bad behaviour should, perhaps, be to do something kind for the person they have upset or angered. Their efforts to make repair should be supported and met with acceptance and approval. Discipline needs to be immediate, quick and lead to a place of moving on together with you.

With all children you could consider the ACT approach:

- **A**cknowledge the behaviour,
- **C**ommunicate the limit, and
- **T**arget an alternative.

For example, 'I know that you are angry because your brother took your toy (A), but we do not hit people in this family (C). If you want to hit something you can hit this cushion over here (T).' This breaks down what has happened for your child so that they can better understand what caused them to lash out. It takes children time to link their thoughts and feelings with their actions, and they need our help to get them there. So when you acknowledge how they felt and why they felt that way you help them understand what caused them to lash out. You are also holding a boundary – while it is okay that they felt angry it is not acceptable to hit people. But we understand that sometimes they feel they want to hit out, so we suggest an alternative such as hitting a cushion. This lets them know that they can hit something, but it must be something inanimate like a cushion so they won't hurt themselves or others.

If/Then is another good discipline structure that also empowers your child to self-correct their behaviour and to take responsibility for any consequences. This one is most effective over the age of five. You explain to your child what will happen if they pursue a particular course of action. For example, 'If you tidy your bedroom now, we can go to the park together this afternoon. But if you leave the mess in your bedroom, we will not go to the park and there will be no TV for the afternoon either. Now you choose.' If your child chooses not to tidy their room you simply say, 'Thank you for letting me know that you do not want to go to the park or watch TV today.' When they complain and try to compensate later on you must hold your boundary by saying, 'I hear that you wish you made a different choice, but you can make better choices tomorrow. Today there is no park or TV because that is what you chose to happen.' This way they cannot moan that you are mean or unfair because they made the choice.

Giving simple **Do-overs** is also a good approach. 'I think you forgot how we do that in this family; would you like a chance to try it again?' If your child behaves appropriately the second time, simply praise their behaviour and move on. If they persist with the negative behaviour, follow through with your consequence or revert to If/Then and break down for them what is about to happen if they keep going.

Remember, a child who needs attention will get it even if it is with negative behaviour; there is a secondary gain in the attention and the intensity of emotions surrounding discipline and punishment. Discipline, especially with a focus on punishment delivered with anger or disapproval, can affect the child's basic sense of security and parent constancy (where a child believes that their parent still loves them, no matter what). It is of vital importance that after correcting the misbehaviour you reconnect positively with your child: 'I don't like this behaviour but I will always love you no matter what you do. It makes me really happy when you behave well and show us your listening/playful/ happy part.' Here you have named the behaviour and not the child as the cause of anger, assured them you still love them and left them with a positive message of what they can choose to do differently. Use as much positive language as you can: 'Three strikes and you're out' is negative enforcement, whereas 'You can do this differently' or 'I believe that you know what to do here' are positive. The aim of discipline is to teach and model for your child how they can internalise the boundaries you have put and held in place, because when boundaries are internalised children feel safe and secure and know that they can protect and control themselves.

Here are some key things to keep in mind.

- Be aware of your child's developmental stage: Ensure your discipline is age and developmentally appropriate.
- Make consequences logical: A child who breaks their toys in temper sees those toys go into the bin and they are not replaced with new ones.
- Make consequences funny and surprising: If your children are fighting, tell them they must do something kind for the other. Perhaps they can make

a snack the other likes or give the other their favorite toy to play with.

- Shine the spotlight on the positive behaviour: Give greater intensity to naming and celebrating what your child does right instead of what they do wrong.

- Be consistent: If you threaten a consequence you must follow through, so be sure that you are happy to do so.

- Give choices where possible: This makes children feel powerful and teaches them decision-making skills.

- Discipline should 'teach' and shape behaviours that you want: Practise the correct behaviour straight away by offering a 'do-over' where the child has the option to correct what they did straightaway and be praised for that behaviour instead of punished for the misbehaviour.

- Use 'I' instead of 'you' when reflecting on the misbehaviour: 'I was angry when you threw your toy at your sister. I hope you can make a better choice next time, I know you can play nicely with your sister by sharing your toys and I feel so happy when you show me that,' instead of 'You were naughty when you threw your toy.'

LYING

A lot of parents talk to me about the issue of how to discipline their children for telling lies. *All* children will tell a lie at some point. I would go so far as to say that lying is as developmental a stage as learning to tell the truth. Children first start to lie around the age of three years old when they suddenly realise that their parents are not mind readers and therefore don't know everything, so they test it out with experimenting with the truth. Examples include 'I've brushed my teeth', 'I haven't had any juice yet today', 'I didn't take a biscuit', etc. Lying will typically increase between the ages of four and six years old but it will take them until about eight years old to refine lying to the extent that they can sometimes get away with it. Before this they tend to get caught or perhaps even own up themselves.

White lies (harmless, mostly told with good intentions to protect the feelings of another) in small doses are okay – from both parents and children. There can also be pro-social benefits to lying. This is when we keep traditions around Santa, the Easter Bunny and the Tooth Fairy alive, generation to generation. These are lies we tell because we care and are associated with doing good and being compassionate.

Essentially view your child lying as another developmental stage that you will parent them through by being calm and consistent, gentle yet firm. When your child lies to you about the small stuff, here are some tips.

- Emphasise the importance of telling the truth in your family. Be far more interested in the truth and almost uninterested in the lie.
- Use paradox by indirectly calling out the lie, but not in a shaming way, for example 'That's a great story you're telling. You are so good at making up stories, I bet you could write a book of stories you've made up.'
- Exaggerate the lie and make jokes – take their lead

and hugely embellish the lie they're telling to make a big joke out of it.

- Praise them for owning up and telling you the truth. Say something like, 'I like it when you're honest,' and focus on that without a consequence for the lie – the important part is that they own up.

- Read books or stories with a life lesson about lying ('The Boy Who Cried Wolf' is the classic one) and ask your child what they thought about the story afterwards. Later, when they lie you can refer back to this story and ask if they remember what happened to the boy who cried wolf.

Now when it is a lie about the bigger and more important stuff you need to address it head on, which does not mean with force.

- Try to reassure them that telling the truth will not get them into trouble.

- Assure them that you can help them with this.

- Talk calmly about the issue, whatever it is – this may mean you have to hear it and say, 'I just need to think about what you've told me for a few minutes and then we can talk some more about it,' to buy yourself time to process and develop a plan.

- If it pertains to their or another's safety you must act on it in the first instance and involve relevant parties.

DE-ESCALATING BEHAVIOUR

Have you ever found yourself exasperated at having to repeat yourself over and over again? Wondering why your child doesn't seem to be able to take in what you are saying or doesn't seem to be listening to you? Of course you have – who among us hasn't?

When a child is in a heightened state of anxiety/anger they are in a state of what we call anticipatory arousal. In this state they are locked into how they are feeling and are simply looking for evidence that they are right to feel the way they do, even if it means acting out, self-sabotaging and making the situation even worse for themselves by inciting your anger and disapproval. In this state you simply cannot reach them with words. When you find yourself exasperated and yelling, 'Did you hear what I said?' the answer is 'No' because they cannot hear you when they are in a hyper-aroused state.

You must find a way to de-escalate the behaviour and allow your child to calm down before trying to reason with them. Try to avoid asking things like, 'Why did you do that?' because they won't be able to explain – they often don't understand it themselves. Instead try, 'I think you kicked the table over because you were feeling upset about X. I'm glad you could show me how you were feeling but I want to help you find a way to show your feelings that won't hurt you or anybody else.' Ultimately the purpose of discipline is to teach your child to control themselves in a variety of environments and circumstances.

This is why we speak about time-in over time-out. Time-outs enjoyed a surge in popularity after particular parenting TV shows highlighted them as a form of managing children's behaviour. But what the TV shows don't show is that time-out works with very few children (a TV show can carefully select participants so that the model will look 100% successful when it isn't). For many children time-out is experienced as a form of rejection; it is a shame-based model and causes them increased anxiety, resulting in increased behavioural difficulties. Now we are seeing a swing the other way, towards a time-in model.

The classic time-out is when a child is directed (verbally or physically) to go somewhere (like the bottom step of the stairs, a chair or facing a wall) alone for a set number of minutes, typically determined by their age, i.e., one minute per year of their age. Parents are encouraged to withhold attention and disregard any cries or requests from the child during a time-out. Time-outs may prevent a behaviour from occurring in the moment but my concern is that they can also make children feel abandoned, rejected, frightened and confused.

Time-in is a positive alternative that is often more effective and helpful for both parent and child. This is when a child who is having a difficult time and acting out is calmly invited to sit near their parent/caregiver, perhaps initially in silence, but then they are asked to express their feelings. Parents should endeavour to empathise with the child's feelings, and often just quiet connection is all that is needed until the moment has passed. Instead of sending them away to be alone, separate them from the rest of the 'action' (if there are other people around), go with them to a quiet room and sit with them, read a book, tell a story, look out of the window (changing visual field can help reset the brain), offer a drink of water, wait with them until they feel better. This is not to say that you let your child continue with a behaviour that is inappropriate. The time-in gives you the opportunity to really connect and then address whatever change needs to be made. As we've seen, what is often interpreted as attention-seeking behaviour is more often a need for connection, and this approach enables that to happen. You need to secure a connection before you move to correction.

It is vital that after correcting the misbehaviour you reconnect positively with your child: 'I don't like this behaviour, but I will always love you, no matter what you do.' Once the situation is calm and you have reflected on the behaviour, move to help them make repair. You can invite the child to do something co-operative with you (like make dinner, play a game, draw with you, etc.). Children are very sensitive/reactive to non-verbal communication. After you have corrected the misbehaviour, make sure your face/body language no longer shows anger/dismay/disapproval.

Repair and recovery are of vital importance in any discipline strategy. Dr Ed Tronick conducted some experiments on breaks in parent–child connection that were quickly followed by positive reconnection[8]. He found that breaks in normal, healthy, secure parent–child relationships were not only positive but were necessary to allow for growth and development. Breaks in the parent–child relationship happen all the time. Think about when your small child starts to crawl and they are so delighted with themselves and this newfound independence as they set off across the room heading straight for the plug socket and its little finger-sized holes. You spot this and from behind them you yell, 'No, stop!' Baby gets a fright and cries and you rush to scoop them up, kiss and hug them, say you didn't mean to frighten them, and redirect them to a safer part of the room. This is very normal and no lasting damage is done. Equally, when your child is older and they seek your attention or want you to come and play with them or look at the masterpiece they have created with their Lego, but you are tied up on the phone or with a pot of boiling food and you say, 'No, not now, I'm busy,' and they walk away dejected and sad, then you finish what you were doing and find them to see what they wanted to show you and you share in their joy and achievement. These are examples of everyday rupture followed by a quick and healthy repair. These kinds of rupture are normal, but rupture that is not followed by repair or leaves a child in a state of prolonged rupture all day can be very damaging to their emotional health.

REWARDS

I have a theory about human behaviour. I believe if we look for the good we will find it. I am not a huge advocate of behaviour charts because they can be experienced by children as shaming since they are hung up for anyone to see when they come into the house. One child told me that she hated the behaviour chart because when Granny visited she would know that she was in trouble just by seeing it on the wall. Also when a child knows that they must earn a sequence of positive marks or stickers in order to be deemed 'well behaved' there is little incentive to recover when they have a bad day in the middle. Further, I worry that we are teaching our children that it is only worthwhile to behave well when there is a reward involved.

Reward charts tend to give quick but short-term solutions to behaviour challenges. This is in large part what makes them so popular with behaviour modification parenting TV shows because the 'expert' can seemingly turn a screaming, tantrumming child into a smiling, compliant child in two short days. But does it last? What makes good TV does not necessarily make long-lasting good parent–child relations. I have often found that while the chart may solve one problem, another behavioural symptom soon emerges in its wake and now there is a second behaviour chart system on-the-go for that behaviour.

Reward charts rely on external motivating factors to change behaviour, but meaningful change will only come from an internal motivation. For this reason I think we have to turn this reward chart approach on its head and start from a place where the child is viewed as 100% good and the challenge is that they *stay* well behaved rather than *become* well behaved.

....

15-minute practice: The behaviour jar

Take a **jar** and fill it with coloured foam pieces/coloured cotton balls or ping-pong balls (marbles are also fine, but be aware of the choking hazard if you have smallies in the house). On one side of the jar stick three lines (use strips of paper or coloured Post-its). You can secure their buy-in to this system by making a big fuss over the jar. Decorate it with your child and clearly explain to them the rewards and consequences. Decorate the jar with their favourite characters or use coloured foam inside that is a mix of colours they love.

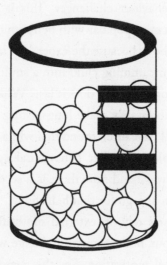

The basic premise is that you believe your child can behave really well, so they start at 100%. Now for each **behavioural transgression** they lose a number of balls/ foam pieces. But they can make repair and recover from this by improving their behaviour in a meaningful way. You can decide with them that if they can behave well for the remainder of the day they can earn these pieces back. You want to catch them doing well so your aim is to support them to stay at the top line.

The idea behind this jar is to have a **visual aid** to go along with house rules and expected behaviour. When your child physically sees the coloured foam going down towards the warning levels, they will immediately associate this with 'I need to make up for those lost pieces.'

If they are at the top line by the end of the week they earn a **privilege**. If they are at the second line they are on a warning and may lose screen privileges for a day – they now know that they have a lot of work to do to catch up; and if they are on the bottom line they lose a privilege.

Do not use 'stuff' as reward or consequence – this just doesn't work. Instead rely on time and privilege. You can have them earn an extra 15 minutes up with you after their usual bedtime as the privilege, or a special movie afternoon with you at the weekend, or special hot chocolate time-in with you one-to-one, for example. Equally you can deduct 15 minutes at bedtime or assign additional chores if they are on the bottom line.

The following week they **start at 100%** again and aim to have another good week or a better week than the one that has finished. Either way, that week is finished and they start afresh now.

CHAPTER 12

Siblings

Our siblings are often our first experiences of friends and enemies and we begin to learn how to manage the dynamics of peer relationships within the sibling dynamic. I am often asked about managing sibling rivalry, closely followed by the question of how a parent can avoid getting pulled into the referee role that only results in one or other child declaring that you always take the side of their sibling. It can often feel as if you just can't win on this one, so this chapter is about exploring ways to creatively manage the rivalrous sibling dynamic, resulting in fewer tears and more laughter for everyone at home.

Sibling rivalry is something most parents who have two or more children will be familiar with. Sibling rivalry is a type of competitive animosity between children in the same family (blood related or otherwise) and by its nature it means that children will oscillate wildly between loving and seemingly hating each other from time to time (sometimes hour to hour). As each child grows and develops their needs change and this impacts greatly on how they feel about each other at different ages and stages of development. However, just because it is quite typical doesn't mean it isn't distressing to hear your children fight with each other because this type of regularly occurring conflict is stressful for everyone, and it is this stress, more than the actual fighting, that will cause you to snap.

An age gap of three years or more significantly reduces the incidence of sibling rivalry, largely because your children will be at different developmental stages to each other and won't have that same need to compete. It is perhaps a little late in the game to glean that nugget of information when your children are already here and already fighting with each other. The same is true when there is an age gap of 12–18 months because the first child hasn't had you to itself quite long enough to view the new sibling as a competitor for your attention and focus. Your first child is still developing a sense of self and 'other-awareness' and (generally speaking) welcomes the new sibling as a convenient playmate. A two-year age gap can often bring the strongest levels of sibling rivalry. This makes sense given that one child will be right in the midst of the so-called 'terrible twos' when the next one is arriving. At this stage of toddlerhood your child is developing a stronger sense of self and expressing increased autonomy, having fully embraced 'No!' and 'Mine!' as their vocabulary of choice. What we call the terrible twos are actually the developmentally very normal and appropriate twos; they're just not very pleasant to deal with, especially when you are also attending to a new baby at the same time. And just as you have the first child moving beyond this competitive/combative toddler stage, the next child is entering it, so you find yourself facing a second rivalrous child working hard to exert their independence. So I'm afraid with a two-year age gap, sibling rivalry may be unavoidable.

Their different and incompatible developmental needs are often the reason siblings fight with each other, but there are other factors at play here too. Sometimes their temperaments are just so similar that they spark against each and rarely seem to get into or stay in sync with each other. One might expect that a laid-back child and a more highly strung child would complement each other's temperaments, each having different needs and response patterns to stress, but if one child presents as needy and not only demands but gets more of your attention as a result, this can irk the other child, who might resent the behaviour of their sibling being rewarded (as they see it) and may even feel that they are losing out on time with you as a result of it.

PLAYING REFEREE

Ideally you do not need to get involved. Yes, that is easier said than done, but you will want to avoid acting as a referee between your children as much as you can, in part because it is frustrating and stressful and often results in more tension as they end up not only frustrated with each other but also with you, but also because you are trying to raise resilient children with strong reflective functioning and problem-solving skills. So you need to get creative in the way you respond.

When you have two children fighting with each other, the ideal is to separate them until they calm down. However, when you send each to their room it is quite difficult at a young age (when they are still learning to self-regulate their emotions) to achieve this; and they may actually sit in isolation percolating all the things they don't like about their sibling, and possibly you, and come out of the room even more enraged. Perhaps try instead to separate them with a task. They must each draw a picture or make a card for the other showing or listing three things that they like about the other person. Once done they exchange the cards/pictures and you all move on. The objective here is to switch their focus from what they do not like about each other to what they do like about each other, which will improve their mood and lower the tension between them. Whether your child gets this done in 10 minutes or two hours is up to them, but it must be done before they can get back to playing.

If they are fighting over something like whose turn it is to choose their TV show or use the games console, or whatever is acting as a trigger, you can sit them down and have them design a schedule that everyone agrees to. Then get them to sign it or perhaps dip their thumb into an ink pad and put their thumb print on it. You stick it up and the next time you hear, 'It's my turn, give it back,' you can draw their attention to the schedule and have them say whose turn it is. If they protest you can reflect how they signed it to say they agreed to abide by it.

These types of strategy help you avoid being pulled in as the baddie or being accused of showing preferential treatment to one over the other, and help these normal sibling tensions to resolve and blow over more quickly.

While sibling rivalry is not pleasant it does come with some good psychosocial benefits and is entirely normal and healthy (for the most part), so we should not rush to pathologise it. Facing and negotiating through conflicts like these equips children with some important life skills as they grow and develop; for example, respect for themselves and others in how they advocate their point of view while considering the situation from their sibling's perspective, even if they don't agree with them. This is fundamental in developing a capacity to compromise and negotiate, which in turn helps us to learn how to manage our anger and aggressive impulses.

Be clear about your expectations regarding how your children should behave together. Make these positive statements that clearly state what you want to see from them, rather than what you don't. For example:

In this family we ...

- Listen to each other
- Speak and act kindly to each other
- Take turns
- Use words to show how we feel
- Help each other
- Work out solutions together
- Take a break from each other when we feel too angry to do any of these things.

You will come up with your own list of positive family rules that work for you. Consider writing them up and sticking them somewhere so that you can refer to them when you need to. Also remember to lead by example – remember that our children take their cues from us. We must always speak kindly to them, even when we are displeased with their behaviour. For example, 'Please don't hit my foot with your train. You can go around me', 'Thank you for listening and playing safely.' It is also important to include the 'take a break from each other' line and to model this ourselves when we need it. It shows children that we all need our own space from time to time and it is a good thing when we can recognise these times for ourselves.

All of this being said, sometimes you will hear yourself default to 'police mode' rather than 'amateur child psychologist mode'. Do not beat yourself up about this – there are times when restating and holding limits is the best way to manage the heated sibling moment. You are not damaging your children's mental health by going into limit-setting mode – far from it! When you are in this mode, try to ensure that you are giving them clear unambiguous messages about what you expect from them and how you expect them to treat each other. Staying calm is the key to success when you are in police mode. You should not have to be loud to be an effective authoritarian.

Remember that humour and creativity will catch your warring children off guard and will often be enough to break the tension and redirect their focus in a calmer and more harmonious way. I was working with a family who had two children aged five and seven, and sibling rivalry was a constant challenge at home. On one occasion when they came to see me I observed that the older child had a noticeable chunk of hair missing from the front of their head. I wondered aloud when they had got the new hairdo. The child immediately launched into a tale of how the other one had 'attacked' them and cut their hair while they slept on the sofa after football practice. Rather than allow the session to turn into a tell-tale narrative that might shame the younger child and reignite the tensions of that moment, I said, 'I wonder if we planted that clump of hair would it grow back?', at which both children laughed and explained that was not how hair grows. All of a sudden we were all talking about how hair grows back and this was not such a big deal. I'm not suggesting you always let such transgressions slide with humour but that you watch for opportunities to do so. This is especially effective if the children tell on each other to the parent who wasn't at home at the time – but the second parent knows that the first parent has already adequately dealt with the issue and there is no need for it to come up again.

Don't sweat the small stuff and know when to pick your battles. Sometimes your children pick on each other and work it out and move on in the time it would have taken you to intervene and discipline someone. Keep an ear open and if the situation escalates or somebody's safety is compromised, of course step in, but when they come to you to fix their fight it is good practice to ask them what they have done to solve the problem themselves. If they say 'Nothing', respond with, 'It sounds like you're not ready for me to step in yet. Go back and try to work this out yourselves first because I am betting you don't need me on this one – you guys are well able to handle something like this,' and let them prove you right.

EQUALITY

Here's a somewhat controversial note ... children do not have to be treated equally. Yes, they will demand that you are fair in how you engage with and respond to them, but this does not translate as treating each of them equally all the time. Allow me to elaborate.

As parents you will hear your children crying, 'That's not fair! It's my turn to press the button in the lift ... He got to go first the last time ... It's her turn to take the rubbish bag out ... She has more crisps than me,' and so on. But the moment you find yourself emptying a packet of crisps onto the table to count them out into separate and even piles *stop it*, because this is one battle you simply cannot win – if only because one child will spot that the other has a crisp that's bigger than any they have in their pile, making it all NOT FAIR again. Your children will always find a way to assert that you treat them differently and each will believe that you show preferential treatment to the others over them. If you are always trying to make things fair you are doing yourself and your children a disservice because in doing so you are inadvertently reinforcing ideals of evaluation, comparison and judgement. So save yourself the headache and embrace the fact that fairness does not mean absolute equality all the time. This is not only an important lesson for us to learn as parents, it is a vital life lesson to teach our children.

It is important to say here that your children may well be correct about these perceptions, at least some of the time, and that's okay. It will prove far more effective for you if you can take the time to clearly communicate your reasons for such differential treatment when it arises. If you explain clearly why one sibling is getting something when the others are not – for example, 'Yes your sister got to have hot chocolate with me while you were playing football with your friends. I love to spend one-to-one time with you all when I can and you and I will have our one-to-one time when she is at her activity' – you will mitigate the bubbling sibling jealousy and even increase the likelihood that your children will begin to see that even differential treatment is fair.

So rather than driving yourself crazy trying to ensure everything is always equal between your children, work on instilling the belief in them that they are all loved and valued and that you have more than enough love to ensure that everyone gets what they need from you. At the same time, we are all different and have different interests, needs and wants, so when one child needs a new pair of runners you will try to get them as soon as you can, but because they need them, not because their sibling just got a pair and you are trying to be 'fair' by getting everyone the same thing at the same time.

We want to reinforce our children's sense of their own unique value and sense of self and we will best achieve this by introducing them to the notion of differential treatment without animosity.

15-minute practice: One-to-one time

I know that achieving one-to-one time with each child is a big challenge when you are parenting young children close in age. We tend to treat them as a herd and force them to be together all day, perhaps even participating in the same activities and playing together. We are all individuals and it is perfectly healthy to need and want time just for yourself. Think in terms of 15 minutes of one-to-one time as often as you can manage it because just a little time with each child can help restore a sense of connection and in turn ease simmering sibling tensions. Try to ensure that for each child you find the activity and/or type of play that best suits them and gives them most joy, and then enable that space for each of them as best you can. This need not be yet another thing that you have to find time for; you can embed one-to-one time into your existing routine.

If you are going through the **car-wash** take one child with you and you have some quality one-to-one time while you are sitting waiting for the wash to be done.

Chat over bath time and catch up on their day (age-dependent, of course).

Make a point of having **dinner or breakfast together** and don't be in a rush. Talk about your day and ask about theirs. Structure this with questions like, 'What was the best bit of your day or what bit do you wish you could change?'

Take an extra 15 minutes to read the **bedtime story** and kiss them goodnight.

When the other child(ren) is at an activity or play date, **maximise your one-to-one time** with your other child. This could even be getting a hot chocolate or simply going for a walk together while you wait to collect the others.

Use your **weekends** to make up for lost time. Try to spend time with each child individually, even if it means one parent taking one child while the other parent takes the others, and rotate this each weekend so each child gets time with each parent.

These small changes will make big differences with ripple effects because when your children feel they have their own time and space with you they will compete for your attention much less. And as this list shows, it doesn't have to be day-long outings to shopping centres – 15 minutes is often enough – because you want it to be sustainable. Consistency and predictability are what matter most here.

CHAPTER 13

Sensitive Children and Uh-Oh Feelings

T he problem with sensitivity is how misunderstood it is in our society. Sensitivity is often used in the context of chastisement: 'Don't be so sensitive, I was joking' or 'Your problem is you're just too sensitive.' But sensitivity can be a wonderful quality to possess. Sensitive people are highly attuned to the emotions and feelings of others. They are good at reading people and situations quickly and have an immense capacity for empathy. All of which are great qualities in any adult and, goodness knows, if we had more sensitive people in the right jobs and positions of power in our society wouldn't we all be much better off?

That said, it can be very difficult to be a sensitive child because sensitive children can easily become emotionally overwhelmed. The reason for this is that it is very difficult for a young child to distinguish between their own emotional experiences and the emotions of another, and of course we cannot process another person's emotional experiences for them, so the child can easily become overwhelmed. It's a little like a sponge that gets saturated and can no longer soak up any more fluid until somebody wrings it out. A somewhat crude analogy perhaps, but sensitive children need help from their parents to process and release what they are feeling so that they can move on unburdened. For this reason, you will find that you need to employ different parenting strategies for your more sensitive children.

EMOTIONS AND ANXIETY

Some more emotionally sensitive children tend to feel things at a 'too much' level. They do not feel sad, but devastated. They do not feel cross, but enraged. They do not feel excited, but hyper. It can be tempting to dismiss their emotional acting-out as 'overreacting' or 'making a mountain out of molehill'. I've heard such children described as 'drama queens' or 'mothers of sorrows' who 'overreact'. This type of expression is unhelpful in parenting such children, who actually need a more empathic parental response from us.

You may need to suppress your inner eye-roll mechanism and instead develop and memorise key phrases that you can default to when you feel tempted to dismiss or minimise their experiences, for example, 'You feel very strongly about this and I can see your sad part is very big right now. I wonder what we can do together to help you with that sad part so that we can make your happy part bigger?' You are acknowledging how they feel while reminding them that this is just one part of them and not all of them. In other words, they might feel sadness now but they are not the sad child in your family. You are also helping them understand that such feeling states are transient, not permanent, and that there are things we can do to process our feelings, which is often easier done with a parent than on their own. In reminding your child of all of this you are also reminding yourself of it, which makes you less likely to say something like, 'Oh, come on, it's not that big a deal – snap out of it.'

When more sensitive children are referred to me for therapeutic work it is often with a presentation of anxiety or stress-related symptoms. These can include (but are not limited to) tummy aches, headaches, sleep disturbance, recurring negative thoughts, fear that something bad will happen to them or someone they know, food refusal, wetting/soiling, irrational fears (e.g. a fear of vomiting or of the wind), clingy behaviour and difficulty concentrating in school. Anxiety is a complex clinical symptom to speak about and explain and I find that it is far easier for children to understand and identify with what I call Uh-Oh feelings.

Something I find very effective is to ask them to picture their Uh-Oh feeling.

- What colour is it?
- What shape and size is it?
- Where does it live in your body?
- Is it heavy or light?
- Is it there all the time or does it only appear some of the time?
- What kind of things makes it feel bigger than usual?
- When was the last time you felt it? Can you tell me the story of that time?

⊕ Can you try to draw/paint it or make it out of clay/ Play-Doh?

It is amazing the insights you will gain into your child's emotional experience of anxiety by gently exploring it in this way. For example, I saw a six-year-old girl who was prone to episodes of explosive rage, seemingly from nowhere – as her parents described it, 'She goes from zero to ninety all of a sudden.' (Nobody goes from 0 to 90. If a child seems to hit 90 all of a sudden, they were not at zero to begin with but probably simmering at about 50–60 all the time, then escalating with minimal provocation. In these situations we need to work out why their 'normal' emotional resting level is so elevated before we can address the spike to 90.)

This six-year-old girl was trying to explain her feelings of rage, but of course that's a very difficult thing to do, especially when you are holding so much rage to begin with. I explored it with her and learned that she had purple triangle feelings that lived in her head. She told me, 'No good comes from these purple triangles and when they are glowing inside me things will get very bad.' She added that she couldn't get them to calm down once they got going. We decided to draw them on pieces of paper, which we then rolled up and pushed inside flat balloons before blowing up the balloons and tying them. We released some balloons out of the window, having talked about the incidents associated with those feelings and deciding that these were ones she could let go of. With others that still needed some time we turned the balloon into a punching bag. Then we used a pin to 'explode' the purple triangle feeling. Emotions are quite abstract for us adults to articulate, explain and process, but they are even more so for our children, especially sensitive children who struggle to discern one emotional state from another. The balloon sequence is highly effective, but so too is the **body map of feelings.**

You will need to get a long roll of paper or wallpaper lining from any hardware shop. Roll it out on the floor and have your child lie on top of it. Cut it to fit their length and then trace an outline around their entire body, talking as you go: 'I am going up your leg, around your ribs and down your arm and all around each finger …' When you have drawn their outline get them to kneel alongside you on the floor looking at the page. Lay out a range of coloured crayons or markers. Name feelings one at a time and ask your child to select a colour for each. For example, you might say, 'What colour is anger?' and they might say 'Black/red'; then ask the same about being happy, Uh-Oh feelings, being excited, sad, confused, etc. Be sure to include a mix of positive and negative feelings and never question the colours they select or assign to a feeling.

Everybody will view or picture their feelings in their own way. I find it helpful to write down a colour/feelings code as we go to make sure I do not forget what they have chosen. Once you have selected a range of feelings (six or seven should be enough; you can always add more later) and chosen the colours you are ready to move on to where these feelings live in their body. Hand them one colour/feeling at a time and ask them to colour in the part of

Happy ☐

Sad ☐

Uh-Oh ☐

Confused ☐

Excited ☐

Angry ☐

the body where this feeling lives. If it's a small feeling they make it small and if it is a pervasive feeling they can colour in a larger area. It is okay for multiple feelings to live in the same place and you should mention this. This will allow you to see if your child stores the majority of their emotions in their head or in their tummy and how this may correlate with tummy aches or headaches/emotional fatigue symptoms. (If your child is complaining of recurring physical symptoms it is always a good idea to bring them to your doctor to have any underlying physical causes confirmed or ruled out.)

You can take this exploration deeper still by wondering about a time when they felt each feeling as they colour it in. Try to be specific, for example, 'I wonder if you can tell me about a time when you had this feeling?' Your aim here is to support your child to identify multiple feeling states, to see that they are made up of a variety of emotions and feelings and that all feelings, good and bad, are healthy and normal. By inviting the stories of times they felt these feelings you are helping them link their emotional states to lived experiences, which will enable them to integrate the learning from the experience and process it better. You can also 'wonder' with them what they now think and feel about these experiences, which will support the development of their reflective functioning capacity – you are helping them see that how they feel now may be quite different from how it felt at the time (e.g., 'At the time I was scared but now I understand that it was just a movie and not real life so I feel okay about it'). When the body map of feelings is complete you can stand together and look at it before deciding to hang it somewhere. I suggest sticking it to the inside of a wardrobe door so that they can see it when they choose to but do not see it all the time.

Remember that our feeling states grow and develop as we do. For this reason I would suggest revisiting the body map of feelings every four to six months and seeing if they would like to do another one to reflect how they are feeling now. Some children will and some won't, and either way it is fine. By inviting them to choose whether or not to do another one you are keeping the feelings conversation door open.

These are helpful, practical and therapeutic ways to support your children to develop an emotional language as they grow. Not all children will want or need to explore their feelings at this level, and certainly not all the time. But our more emotionally sensitive children may actually *need* to do so and may require our support and help to bring them to a place of being able to process emotional states, even if they don't particularly want to because it is difficult – and don't we all tend to avoid difficult tasks?

SELF-HOLDING CHILDREN

Some children tend towards more 'self-holding' strategies when they are dealing with emotions and distressing experiences. Self-holding is a term that was developed by the child psychoanalyst Donald Winnicott to describe a pattern of behaviour in children who choose to try to deal with their difficult feelings on their own rather than reaching out to others to help them. They have either always coped this way or have stopped reaching out to others for some reason. Self-holding strategies may work well for many children, at least most of the time, but it can be very difficult for them to seek support from others even when their own attempts to resolve what is going on have failed and they really need help from you. These are the *grin and bear it* children. It will often look as though they are coping very well, but if you were to scratch the surface you would see more of their emotional turmoil bubbling just beneath the surface. I came across such a child when I was invited into a school to offer support to a class of seven-year-olds when one of their classmates had died. The teacher gave me a list of names of children she was most concerned about, many of whom had already been displaying so-called challenging behaviour before this tragedy struck. In doing so she added as she passed over a name on the class list, 'I'm certainly not concerned about this child; she is the happiest girl in the school. She's won an award for it.' This stopped me in my tracks and I said, 'Excuse me, say that again, she has won an award for happiness?' The teacher explained that this child was happy and smiled all day every day in school. Never gave cause for concern but quietly and calmly went about her work. At student awards day at the end of the previous academic year, she was awarded a certificate for being the happiest child in the school. My response was simple: 'I will start with her.'

It is not normal to be happy all day every day. We are human and we are designed to experience and express a wide range of emotion in our day-to-day lives. A child who shows only one emotion, and a positive appeasing one at that, all the time would raise a flag for me as to where all their other emotional experiences are held. My gut instinct proved correct. This child was terribly distressed at the loss of her classmate, was terrified that she too, or her siblings or parents, could die, was confused about the permanence of death and needed support in processing all of this. But because she was a self-holding child, she needed someone to see beyond and beneath her smile because she couldn't reach out herself for help with her feelings.

It is not as simple as self-holding children 'bottling feelings up', because it very often will not even occur to them to share their feelings with anyone else. They might even feel that sharing their feelings would result in them feeling worse or perhaps shamed about how they feel. Such children need help to develop an emotionally expressive language that will enable them, slowly and in a non-threatening way, to open up about their feelings. This language will likely not be a verbal one.

Here are a few techniques that I have found helpful when working with self-holding children. While these techniques are therapeutic, they can be easily used in a non-therapeutic way by parents at home with very positive outcomes.

For the **sand bottle of feelings,** you will need:

- A bottle or jar (plastic or glass are fine but be sure you have a lid to seal the top)
- Different colours of sand (you can also use plain/ white sand and colour stain it with coloured chalk in your hands – it's a little messier but it works if coloured sand is not an option)
- A funnel or piece of paper.

Have the coloured sand in separate containers and either use a funnel or create a funnel with a rolled piece of paper. Invite your child to assign a different feeling to each colour and now have them *pour their feelings* into the bottle. If one feeling feels bigger for them, they should reflect this by using more of that colour in the bottle. Have them continue until the bottle is full (it's important it is full so that the sand won't mix should the bottle shake or fall) and put the lid on top (if you have no lid, you could seal the top by pouring in melted wax – but since this is hot and potentially dangerous, take appropriate precautions). What you now have is a very attractive bottle with layers of different-coloured sand and that is simply how it will look to anyone else who might see it, but to your child it is a visual representation of their internal emotional world.

An alternative to this approach is to make **feelings jewellery** with your child. You will need:

- Coloured beads (you can get these in craft/hobby shops or in children's jewellery-making kits)
- Thin elastic
- Plastic needle (for threading – if the beads have wider holes you may not need this).

Invite your child to assign a feeling to each colour. They then thread how much of each feeling they experience onto the elastic. When they've finished you tie a knot or attach a clasp. They can make a feelings necklace or bracelet or both. The added advantage of making a bracelet with elastic is that they can wear it on their wrist and if/when they feel their Uh-Oh feelings rising up they can gently yet firmly pull on the elastic bracelet on their wrist. Feeling it pull on their wrist will bring their focus to the bracelet, which will serve to remind them that they are made up of a mix of feelings and these Uh-Oh feelings are just one feeling. This will often help bring them back out of their heads and into the moment, which will help calm and contain them and regulate their emotions in the moment when they might not be with you for you to help them with it.

I say to do these activities *with* your child because of course they could manage these activities on their own (especially if they're close to seven years old), but doing them in the presence of a witness is more beneficial and comforting. They are about feelings, and you are there to bear witness as your child processes their feelings. You don't query or approve their expression ('Really? Yellow for angry? Isn't that a happy colour? I think red is better for anger'). This is not your process; it is theirs. You can reflect their effort or simply observe quietly as they work. Saying things like 'I can see you put a lot of thought into what colour your feelings are,' is more appropriate.

Self-holding or bottling up feelings is not only stressful; it is also very hard work. The effort to contain everything inside is exhausting and requires much more focus and effort than sharing those feelings would. The developing brain will seek to release this tension by pushing the child to unburden themselves emotionally, but without successful strategies this pent-up emotion will be released in the form of challenging behaviour or emotional symptoms (disrupted sleep, disrupted eating patterns, regression in toilet training, difficulty in concentrating, crying, shouting, hurting oneself or others, withdrawal, clumsiness, irrational fears, etc.).

Feelings are messy and many children, for a variety of reasons, do not want to risk showing their internal mess. But having someone who loves us and who we love see our mess and know that they love us anyway, mess and all, is essential to a happy and healthy childhood. But supporting your child to find new and healthier ways to express their emotions is liberating and frees them up to engage far better with their lives, their peers, their activities and their families. As one previously self-holding child (a boy of six) explained to me, 'My sister asked me what I come to see you about so I told her that it was like Feelings Physio and that I had *a knot in my feelings* that you were helping me work out.' I don't think there's a better way than that to describe this process.

NIGHTMARES

Nightmares and bad dreams are tricky and sensitive subjects to explain to your child. Understanding their descriptions of unconscious visuals can be hard to decipher and explaining that these pictures are completely unreal is challenging.

Having your child's room decorated in a way that they like or, even better, a way that they have been involved in choosing, can add to their sleeping experience. Sleeping can often be challenging in general for kids, specifically when they are on their own in their bedroom and separated from you.

When your child comes into your bedroom looking for comfort after a scary dream, walk with them back into their own room and lie with them for a while. Reassure them that they are safe, check for the monsters, read a book or sing them a song until they are peacefully asleep again.

I want to differentiate between a nightmare and a night terror, as they are quite different.

Nightmares usually happen in the middle of a child's sleep, certainly after they have been asleep for a few hours. Often the child remembers the dream, sometimes in vivid detail, and they will know that they had a bad dream and talk about having had it, even if they don't remember it in detail. Some groaning or whimpering accompanies nightmares and tossing/turning is also possible, but they would not normally thrash around in bed, scream, yell, run around or sleepwalk. Because the nightmare dreamer recalls that they had a bad dream and how it felt, with or without detail, they benefit from talking about it with you, perhaps reflecting on what it might mean to them or what might have caused it.

Night terrors, on the other hand, happen during the first few hours of sleep. They are accompanied by loud yelling or screaming and thrashing in the bed and it can be difficult to fully wake the child (though they can be partially awake and still in the night terror), and when you do wake them, the child will rarely remember much, if anything, of the dream. When this happens, try to engage the child in talking about the sensation they felt rather than what happened. They can sometimes recall an overwhelming sensation or perhaps one small scene or a character in the dream sequence. However, most often they do not remember anything at all from the dream and may even be surprised when you mention it the next day, or they may ask you, 'Why did you wake me up?'

It is not really known what causes night terrors in young children, and usually they disappear by puberty, though there are cases of adults experiencing them. These cases can usually be linked directly to periods of high-level stressful daytime situations and they disappear when the stress is dealt with. They can run in families – if a parent experienced night terrors, a child may have an increased risk of experiencing them. They are generally transient and children outgrow them by around seven years old. You can observe your child for possible anxiety behaviours, such as a sudden change in appetite, becoming withdrawn or quiet, becoming upset when going to or coming home from school, or any sudden unexplained changes in behaviour. But sometimes there is no apparent trigger for a night terror – they just happen.

While many professionals will simply suggest you ride it out and that there is no treatment, one approach that has proven successful for *some* families is:

- Let the child fall asleep completely.
- Wake the child, fully-fully awake, after three to five minutes of being fully asleep.
- Wash the child's face with a cold face cloth to ensure that they are fully awake.
- Now settle the child and put them back to sleep again.

Doing this can alter the abnormal sleep patterns of the in-between sleep and awake state and prevent the night terror. It's a technique that can trick the brain into thinking it has been asleep and awake and this can be enough to break the pattern that results in the night terror. However, if you are concerned about sleep disturbance in your child you should seek professional advice.

Nightmares and/or recurring bad dreams can be a traumatic experience for a child and will affect their sleep pattern and routine. Your child may be reluctant to go to bed, say they're not tired, wake themselves up in the early hours and need reassurance during the night. So here is a tried and tested technique to address children's nightmares or bad dreams that *always* works! Being supremely confident about this is a key part to the success of this technique.

If your child experiences a nightmare or recurring bad dreams, set aside a block of time the next day to sit with them. Ensure that you have *uninterrupted time*: 15 minutes should be enough time but allow up to 30 minutes, to give this your full attention. You will need paper (two sheets), markers or crayons/pencils.

Sit down with your child and tell them that you know a way of stopping bad dreams that always works. Be supremely confident in how you sell this! Invite them to think about the bad dream and to draw the bit of the dream that scares them most. Reflect on what you see in this drawing without projecting your own thoughts, for example, 'I see this black bit here, I wonder what that is.' The use of 'wondering' can help your child go deeper into the dream but it doesn't put pressure on them if they don't want to – a direct question can put pressure on them to produce an answer.

Tell them that dreams are exactly like movies and that they are the director of their dream so they can decide to yell 'Cut!' and change the scene. Have them look at the scary drawing and yell 'Cut!' Now invite them to think about how they would like the dream to go. What would they like to happen instead of this scary bit that would make it a happier dream? Have them visualise the happier change, what it looks like, how it feels, etc.

When your child has the new scene in mind, have them draw this new scene for the dream. Again, reflect on what you see, using 'wondering' to encourage them to talk about this happier scene. Now tell your child that they can tear up the scary part and throw it away and go with them as they bring the new happy dream scene into their bedroom. They can either pin it to the wall by their bed so that they see it every night or place it under their pillow, whichever they prefer. Again, reiterate that this *always* works, so the bad dream won't come back again.

The dream itself is important – it is your child's way of unconsciously processing thoughts during the night – so it is equally important that you spend some time during this process reflecting and wondering with them about the bad or scary parts of the dream. This enables them to put words and feelings to what is happening and to bring it from their unconscious to their conscious thinking, which allows them to process it and let it go. The happier drawing empowers them to believe that they can change the dream, take control of it and change the ending, ultimately reaffirming that when something is scary, they can discuss it with you, think about it, talk about changing the scary thing and then let it go of it. It also allows you and your child to enjoy a restful sleep again.

This technique doesn't mean that your child will never have another bad dream, but it can be used again and again as necessary. It is particularly effective when a child is experiencing a recurring dream. If there is a pattern of recurring and/or frequent bad dreams it may indicate an underlying anxiety, in which case you might want to consider seeking professional advice/support from a child psychotherapist/play therapist/psychologist.

15-minute practice: Just dance

Sometimes you just have to *dance the moodies away!* This is my version of 'just shake it off' or 'just leave it at the front door', whatever phrase suits you. Being separated from each other all day is stressful and sometimes that leftover stress bubbles over at the point of reunification, so instead of being greeted at the door with hugs and kisses and 'Mum/dad is home!', you are walking into a warzone of 'He took my ...', or 'She hit me.' Nobody wants their first interaction with their children after a long day apart to be stern words and consequences, so before you do or say anything, drop your coat and bag and turn on some music so that everyone (yes, everyone) can just *dance their moodies away!* Have some upbeat, happy dance music ready by creating a playlist that you can simply switch on in the moment you need it.

This can be a creative and unexpected response to fighting children but can also be used with more anxious or self-holding children who might find it hard to tell you what they are feeling but still need to work it out. Dancing with you will make them smile and laugh and bring in some of those badly needed endorphins or happy hormones that will serve to break the tension and distract them. After you have danced for a full song you can end up by making a human train and bringing them all with you to the table where you quickly assign duties to help set the table while you start checking in with everyone's best bit of their day and what bit they'd like to change.

It might sound silly but it really does work ... and silly is okay too.

....

CHAPTER 14

Screen Time

You can't avoid screen time, but you can manage it! Just as the development of the postal system for written letters brought the poison pen letter and the chain mail letter; just as the development of a telephone system brought with it hoax/prank calls; mobile phones, screen-based devices, the Internet and new technological advances also bring with them a whole new range of risks and dangers ... along with exciting and important benefits!

A study conducted by mobile technology company Nokia found that, on average, mobile phone users check their phones every six minutes, or up to 150 times a day[9]. At the Paediatric Academic Societies' annual meeting in San Diego in April 2015, researchers cited that more than one-third of babies start using smartphones and tablets before they learn how to walk or talk.[10] Furthermore, more than 50% of children under the age of one year had watched a full TV show, 36% had touched or scrolled a screen and 25% had made a phone call themselves.

Screen-based technology is here to stay, but it is incumbent upon us parents to guide and safeguard our children online and this includes recognising how young is too young and how long is too long to be online. Someone once described to me how their one-year-old child would crawl over to the TV at home, pull themselves up in front of it and try to swipe the screen with their finger as though it were a phone or tablet. The person telling me this marvelled at how quickly young children understand how screen devices worked and thought it was very cute. But is it cute? Or is it worrying that such a young child had already observed, experienced and internalised how to interact with screens? Monitoring your children's usage and engagement with these devices is important and you can achieve this without infringing on their right to privacy.

TRUST AND RISKS

A smart device is not the same as a diary or journal and does not come with the same expectation of privacy. There is a significant difference between a diary and a phone or tablet device. While a diary is a private and personal log of our inner thoughts and feelings that is not shared with anyone else and doesn't involve messages from other people, a WiFi-enabled device is anything but. A WiFi-enabled device involves public messaging and puts our children into contact with other people, even strangers, while exposing them to a wide and varied range of images and information. For this reason, monitoring young children's online behaviour and relationships is very important and is a parental responsibility.

Ideally you should not need to check their devices in a secretive or clandestine manner – if you don't trust them to use the device safely they really shouldn't be allowed to have one. But when you are setting up your rules and expectations with them, in advance of them being given such a device, you can include an understanding that you will sit with them weekly to review their usage. This means that you sit *with* your child and have them talk you through and show you how they have been using the device and/or social media that week. If you notice regular communication between your child and a person whose name you do not recognise, ask more questions about who this person is and take a look at their profile information. If you feel you are not being given satisfactory answers or explanations you will need to ask to see more of the messages they have shared with this person and view the history on the device. It is worth contextualising this for your child that you are not breaching their trust or right to privacy but it is your job to keep them safe and if you are worried you have to act on this.

Giving your children access to a WiFi-enabled device is a way of communicating with them that you trust them to use the device safely and responsibly. If you do not believe this, do not give them the device. If you are considering giving your child a WiFi-enabled device, it can be very useful to gradually expose them to your mobile phone or tablet at home in your presence so that you can see the effects that time on these devices has on them as well as observing how they interact with the device. This is a useful and practical way for you to assess if they are ready to use such a device of their own responsibly. It is also a great way to determine their level of knowledge, not only of the device but also of the platforms and apps, and what kind of apps hold their attention and draw them in. You could also have them talk you through the capacity of your phone/tablet so that you can assess their existing level of knowledge about the capacity of this technology. This will alert you to how little you know in comparison, or if they need more guidance and direction as to the potential uses of the device.

The best way to protect your children from risks posed by technology is to make discussing them a part of your parent–child relationship. You can speak with your children in age-appropriate language about the benefits and the risks of technology. You don't want to frighten them but you do want to inform them in a developmentally appropriate way. Thankfully the majority of children will not encounter a predator online but it is no harm to ensure they know what they should do if they do receive contact that makes them uncomfortable.

Remember that our goal is for our children to be able to engage with technology in an independent, safe and responsible way, so we work towards giving our children increasing levels of responsibility in line with their developmental stage. This might include giving them responsibility for managing their own phone credit out of fixed pocket money – when the credit is gone, they must wait until next week – and they will gradually get better at budgeting.

However, such measures are certainly easier with older children, which brings up the question of whether or not it is at all suitable for younger children to even have access to or possession of such devices.

AGE RESTRICTIONS

In general, children under seven years old do not need to have a mobile phone of their own. I would strongly advise that they do not have one. In some families mobile phones for children can be a very important parenting tool, especially if you are separated from your partner and co-parenting the children. Mobile phones can be useful to stay in touch with your child as to who will pick them up, when and where, or, if your child is delayed after school, to let you know in advance so that you are not worried. In these instances a basic functioning non-smart phone should suffice and once you are reunited with your child they hand you over the phone.

But ultimately this is a parental decision. When you are met with 'All my friends have one', remember that you are only responsible for your own children and their access and behaviour online. That said, I do have some recommendations, stemming from my own professional experiences with young children, about access to and usage of WiFi-enabled devices for under-sevens.

Under three years old: No access to screen-based/WiFi-enabled devices. None at all. The reason for this is that very young children's brains are developing so quickly that they need right-here, right-now, real-world experiences. It is a time of sensory play and exploration. The neuroplasticity of their brains is such that they are soaking up every single piece of stimulus we expose them to and we want them doing so in a developmentally beneficial way. Screen-based devices are not helpful to early brain and emotional development.

Three to five years old: Very limited access that is closely monitored and supervised by parents/caregivers. There is a reason that cartoon episodes are around five minutes long and they are not intended to be streamed back to back. The attention span of a child of this age is very short and they should be moving quickly from one activity to another. This age is also when they should be engaging in projective and narrative-based play, working out social scenarios and solutions for themselves, not watching TV characters doing this. Think along the lines of 5–10 minutes of screen activity with a maximum of 20–30 minutes a day to support optimum development at this age.

Five to seven years old: Gradually increase the level of access within your comfort zone and what you know to be suitable for your child's development and capacity. In saying this I would still strongly advise you carefully monitor and limit screen-based activity at this age. Children are negotiating three crucial stages of developmental play right up to the age of seven years and, as we discussed in Chapter 5 on developmental play, it is only by doing so that they can successfully begin to self-regulate their own emotional states. Prolonged screen usage actively sabotages these stages of play and can serve to short-circuit the natural developmental pathways and catapult your child forward without them having acquired the important benefits these play stages provide them with. The optimum exposure to screens now will differ from child to child, but in general think 30–45 minutes of screen-based activity (really trying to stay under the hour mark as much as you can) and ideally no longer than 20 uninterrupted minutes. Remember, everything 'pauses' these days, so you can get them to pause what they are viewing to help you with a task that involves person-to-person interaction and in-the-moment engagement for about ten minutes before they go online again.

SCREENS AND MELTDOWNS

Something I often hear from parents is that their young child experiences 'meltdowns' when they come to the end of or soon after screen time. This is your child's way of showing you that they had become over-stimulated and could not regulate the level of arousal they were experiencing, so they melt down emotionally. They cannot control this meltdown when it is happening; it is up to us to observe what is and is not working for them and put limits and boundaries in place about usage for them. It is worth noting here that a meltdown is quite different from a temper tantrum.

A temper tantrum is a performance and requires an audience/witness. It is usually in direct response to something that has just happened, i.e., not getting what they want or challenging a boundary or limit you are putting into place. It is (usually) quick enough and the child has some degree of control over it and can bring it to an end themselves or with some guidance and direction from you.

A meltdown is something else entirely. With a meltdown your child is sensorily over-stimulated to the point that they reach their limit. This means that they cannot co-regulate with you, let alone self-regulate their level of arousal. They have little to no control over the meltdown once it starts and it will be very difficult for you to reach them with words or verbal direction. All you can do is to be physically available, try to stay calm, and as soon as you can get them into your arms to use physical touch/rocking/swaying and a soft voice to try to connect with them so that they can co-regulate with you. If you notice that your child is prone to regular meltdowns when they have been occupied with a screen-based device, you might want to reconsider their access to such devices or at least the duration/regularity of their access to them.

The phrase *wired but tired* is appropriate here when your child presents as agitated/hyper-stimulated but also exhausted. If you do suspect that your child fits this category and have observed a pattern that screen time triggers impulsive/defiant/enraged behaviour, you may wish to trial a screen time fast: remove access to all screen devices for a period of two weeks and observe if there is any relief in the symptoms. A break like this can be enough to reset the nervous system that has become over-stimulated. You should also observe a return of their interest in other play activities such as creative and imaginative play and/or time outdoors exploring nature.

Because children's brains are still so malleable and are developing so fast, they respond much more sensitively to screen-based stimulation than adults do. I have worked with many parents who feel that if their child is engaged with others online (as in the case of interactive gaming) it is less harmful than if they were engaged in isolation. This is not the case and for many children this interactive engagement can be even more arousing for young brains, leading to higher levels of emotional dysregulation and prolonged hyper-arousal.

What tends to happen is our children are quiet and occupied on their device and we are getting our own tasks done. Then suddenly we realise that they have been staring into a screen device for over an hour and we rush in and abruptly take the device away. Our child responds with a screeching meltdown and we move into restriction mode, citing their behaviour as evidence that they should not be on the device any more. What has happened here is that we have allowed them to become over-stimulated and hyper-aroused from prolonged and uninterrupted usage. Then we gave them no notice that this time was coming to an end. Time is an abstract notion for children and when we warn '15 more minutes', we may as well say 'two weeks' for all the sense it makes. Similarly, saying that when the clock on the oven 'bings' their time is up feels like the countdown happens *to* them rather than *with* them. But if you use a visual aid like a 15-minute sand timer they get to see their time going gradually and this serves to help them regulate and anticipate the ending coming.

Note: Set up a rule that only adults can touch the timer – or children will turn it back again – and place it somewhere where they can see it but not reach it. These timers are useful in lots of settings such as ending play dates; time in a play centre; bedtime; homework; time to get ready and leave the house, etc.

LEAD BY EXAMPLE

Be aware of your own screen usage too. Remember that our children are looking to us for guidance as to how to behave and they take their emotional lead from us. So if every time they look up at us they see our gaze occupied in a screen they are learning that this is an acceptable way to behave and that screens are super-interesting and all-consuming.

I read an article about a Californian mother who decided to monitor the number of times her young infants sought out her gaze during their playtime. Instead of passing the time on her smartphone while her children played, she sat and watched them at play. Of this experience, she wrote, 'As I sat quietly in the corner of the room I tallied how many times they looked at me for various reasons: to see if I saw their cool tricks, to seek approval or disapproval for what they were doing, and to watch my reactions.' She went on to wonder what kind of message she would have been sending her children had she missed all their attempts to seek out her gaze during their playtime, and how they might have interpreted her inattentiveness. During her experiment on this particular afternoon she counted 28 separate instances when her two-year-old children looked up at her during their play to seek out her gaze.[11]

In Chapter 3 I described how important it is that our gaze meets our young children's gaze, how they look up seeking out eye contact and connection with us from early infancy. Well, if every time, or even most of the time, our children look up at us seeking our gaze and are instead met with the lens of a smartphone, they cannot make the connection they need. They cannot connect with that lens and that lens does not reflect back a positive, warm, loving sense of self to them. We need to put the smartphones away and use our 'eye cameras' to see, connect with and reflect back an emotional sense of self to our young developing children while also modelling for them that person-to-person interaction is more meaningful, pleasurable and enjoyable than screen-based engagement.

15-minute practice: Online awareness

Most children will never experience a problem online and, while there are risks to technology use, there are also benefits and it is important your child is familiar with technology and its uses. If you make them aware of the potential risks and what you expect from them in their Internet/device usage and keep clear and open lines of communication about it, you can trust that they will come to you if and when there is a problem.

- **Inform Yourself**: Take 15 minutes to inform yourself about the capacity of the smart device you are thinking about handing your child. You can look the details up online or seek a consultant in a technology store who will be happy to educate you about the capacity of a device.

- Build up your knowledge of what your children are accessing and what they might be exposed to. Build up your knowledge and understanding of computers, games consoles and mobile phones and what access these devices are giving your child. Research what parental control software is available (and what apps such controls do not work on) and what is best for you and your children.

- **Set rules for safe usage**: Take 15 minutes to sit with your child and agree some ground rules about how the device is to be used. Be comfortable in setting and sticking to rules for what you consider to be safe usage in your family. Involve your children in writing up these rules. Agree that they will come to you if and when they receive something inappropriate online. Make sure your child understands their responsibility for safe usage as well. Explain from the outset that you will be asking them about their usage and that you expect them to be open with you about it. Explain that you are in charge of Internet usage and that if you feel it is not being used appropriately you will prohibit access to it. Place the computer in a family room and ensure all devices are left downstairs at bedtime. Try to make these rules positive in wording, e.g., 'We only share photos with people we know well in real life and we are always fully dressed in those photos,' versus 'Do not share naked photos of yourself.' I like the Granny rule: 'Ask yourself before you hit post if you would be happy for Granny to see this photo or read this message' – if you're not, do not post it. Another positive rule is 'We only post things that are true and that are kind.'

- **Communicate openly about it**: Take 15 minutes each week to sit with your child and have them show you what they have been doing online/on their smart device that week. Ask questions that show interest and curiosity rather than suspicion. Regularly ask your child about their Internet usage, what they are looking at, what they spend most of their time online doing, what they think are the pros and cons of Facebook/instant messaging. Ask if they've ever come across something inappropriate and what they did about it. Share newspaper articles highlighting the dangers with them. Also speak about the benefits and how the Internet can be and is a good thing and how it can help them. Tell them that if they come across anything online that gives them an Uh-Oh feeling they should come straight to you and show you. Be clear you will help them understand it better and they will not be in trouble.

- **Give your child responsibility**: Take 15 minutes to invite your child to show you how to do something on your smart device. This is a good opportunity to give your child some additional responsibilities and to show them that you trust them to use the Internet safely, while at the same time they are showing you how much they know and what the capacity of the device is. Sharing information in this way helps you to stay engaged.

- **If you discover a problem**: Take 15 minutes to gather your thoughts and plan your response. Remember it is best if you respond rather than react! Stay calm. Don't panic. Your child is going to need your help and support and you cannot provide this if you are panicking. Whatever the issue is, first discuss it with your child and give them a chance to explain the matter or to offer suggestions as to how to solve it. Explain that your child will not lose out on privileges or access to the Internet because of the actions of others. If the issue is bullying, you may need to involve other parents and possibly the school. If it is pornography and/or child abuse or grooming, you may need to speak with a child protection agency and the police about it. If you feel your child is too young to discuss these topics with, they are too young to be given access to the device to begin with.

AFTERWORD

Preparing for the Next Stage

Now that you have parented through the first seven years it is time to audit what you need to do to grow your parenting in anticipation of the next stage because just as you have this parenting gig nailed they only go and grow up a stage and you find yourself scrambling to make sense of it all over again.

Between the ages of eight and 12 years, children are still developing their social skills, learning how to interact with peers while trying to understand what others expect from them socially and emotionally. Their play is also evolving and is becoming more intricate. You will still see evidence of magical, fantasy and imaginative play (cops and robbers, time travellers, witches and wizards, etc.), but you will see it take place within larger group play than before and the group will decide (via rotating leadership) who plays what roles in any given play. You will also observe that your girls are playing differently from your boys. Girls' friendships tend to be more intimate, with more examples of playing in close pairs, whereas boys' friendships and peer interactions tend to be less intimate and more group-oriented. (These are generalisations and of course some children will play differently from these gender types.)

It is also at this age/stage of development that children are able to consider situations from the perspective of others on their own and without your prompt. They can reflect on what intention is behind their (and others') thoughts, actions, choices and decisions and because of this they begin to show themselves to be capable of being unkind or mean. Most children will experiment with this thought and behaviour process and while you may fear that your child has become a bully, we must be careful not to pathologise such behaviour and label it inaccurately. What might look at a glance like bullying behaviour is more likely to be their clumsy and inexperienced attempt to show leadership and try to influence others to bring about a particular outcome for themselves.

From a parenting point of view one of the main adjustments you now need to make is to allow for more independence. It can be difficult to accept that your child is growing up and seeking to do more for themselves and make choices without your direction, but this is actually a positive step towards developing autonomy and a stronger sense of self. Now you must take a deep breath and trust that what you have given and done for them this far will stand to them as they take further steps in the world and assert their independence. Of course I am not suggesting that you cut them loose and let them off into the big world alone, but this is a time when you must find opportunities for them to safely practise independent thinking, feeling and choice. Stay focused on their efforts over outcomes and be available to support them to process these experiences whether they go positively or negatively. Your role is not to judge or instruct but more to reflect and encourage them to dust themselves off and try again.

Maintaining your 15 minutes of playful connection each day while practising small but consistent acts of independence now will help them as they prepare to move into adolescence, but it can be hard to let them do so when your instincts are to hold them close and protect them for ever. At the next stage of development your child may dismiss 'play' as being for little kids and feel it no longer applies to them. It is up to you to find creative ways to keep a playfulness in your relationship even if it is not actual play like you used to connect with them. For example, refer back to games like thumb or arm wrestling but consider increasing the level of challenge now that they are older by covering your hands in lotion. Your pre-teen child may not want to hold your hand but they will thumb wrestle or allow you to give them an at home mini manicure/pedicure and this is playful nurture-based connection.

As your child reaches the end of the period from infancy to seven years, set yourself a couple of goals to prepare you for the next stage.

- Always encourage them to play.
- Encourage imaginative and creative thinking; it helps them work out solutions to problems they will encounter as they grow.

- Identify opportunities to practise small but consistent types of independence – this will help them assert themselves in a confident yet respectful way with others.
- Give them areas of their life (including at home with you) when they can show leadership, and praise efforts over outcomes.

They will still need you and depend upon you a lot, so be as available as you can be, but it is vital that your parenting grows up as they do. Trust your children and trust that you have been – and continue to be – good enough.

NOTES

1   Beckes, L., Coan, J. A., and Hasselmo, K. (2013). Familiarity promotes the blurring of self and other in the neural representation of threat. *Social Cognitive and Affective Neuroscience* 8(6) 670–677.

2   Fonagy, P., et al. (2002). *Affect Regulation, Mentalization and the Development of the Self.* New York: Other Press.
    Fonagy, P. et al. (1991). The capacity for understanding mental states: the reflective self in parent and child and its significance for security of attachment. *Infant Mental Health Journal* 13, 201–218.

3   Duke, M. P., Lazarus, A., and Fivush, R. (2008). Knowledge of family history as a clinically useful index of psychological well-being and prognosis: A brief report. *Psychotherapy Theory, Research, Practice, Training* 45, 268–272.

4   Lahad, M. (1992). Storymaking in assessment method for coping with stress. In S. Jennings (Ed.). *Dramatherapy theory and practice II* (pp. 150-163). London: Routledge.

5   Bratton, S. C. et al. (2006). *Child Parent Relationship Therapy (CPRT) treatment manual: A 10-session filial therapy model for training parents.* New York, NY: Routledge.

6   These four dimensions are part of the Theraplay therapeutic model. More information at www.theraplay.org.

7   O'Neal, E., Plumert, J., and Peterson, C. (2016). Parent–Child Injury Prevention Conversations Following a Trip to the Emergency Department. *Journal of Pediatric Psychology* 41(2), 256–264.

8   Tronick E.Z. et al. (1978). The infant's response to entrapment between contradictory messages in face-to-face interaction. *Journal of the American Academy of Child & Adolescent Psychiatry* 17:1–13.

9   2010. Proceedings of the 14th International Academic Mindtrek Conference: Envisioning Future Media Environments. ACM, New York, NY, USA.

10 Kabali et al. (2015). 'First Exposure and Use of Mobile Media in Young Children'. Presented at the PAS annual meeting, San Diego.

11 Bologna, C. (2015). Mom's 'Viral Experiment' Urges Parents to Rethink Screen Time. *Huffington Post.* Available at: http://www.huffingtonpost.com/entry/moms-viral-experiment-urges-parents-to-rethink-screen-time_us_563b7247e4b0307f2cac4020).